Ask a Pastor!

Ask a Pastor!

Biblical Answers to Real-Life Questions

By DANIEL WAIDE

RESOURCE *Publications* · Eugene, Oregon

ASK A PASTOR!
Biblical Answers to Real-Life Questions

Resource Publications
An Imprint of Wipf and Stock Publishers
199 W. 8th Ave., Suite 3
Eugene, OR 97401

www.wipfandstock.com

PAPERBACK ISBN: 979-8-3852-0667-4
HARDCOVER ISBN: 979-8-3852-0668-1
EBOOK ISBN: 979-8-3852-0669-8

VERSION NUMBER 051424

Have a question you'd like answered but can't find it here?
Send it in an email to askapastorfcc1@outlook.com

CONTENTS

INTRODUCTION

Greetings,

I wonder very much what led you to pick up the book you now hold in your hands. Was it a passing interest? The recommendation of a friend? More importantly; what would you like to learn from it?

We live at a time in this country when more and more people are unfamiliar with Christian teachings, or anything to do with church or religion. There is a growing gap between churchgoers and nonchurchgoers in regards to moral perspectives, life expectations, and answers to life's most fundamental questions. Often the questions that people most want answered about God, the Bible, Church, and Christians are ones that we are afraid to ask, for fear of being dismissed as ignorant or "unreligious." These are the questions that we wanted to address in this book.

Roughly two years ago I partnered with a man in my church to offer a weekly news article that addressed any question anyone wanted to ask about God, church, or the Bible. Questions could be submitted anonymously and we sought to present answers that were simple, clear, and straight from the Bible. We had several goals in mind for this project. The first was to connect the life-changing Truth of God's Word to those who sincerely wished for it. The second was to encourage those who are familiar with God's Truth to reexplore it, live it out, and share it with others. We have now collected many of the articles that have been written and are making them available in book form for the first time.

Most of all, our desire has been to introduce this generation to the benefits of belonging to a godly church with a good pastor. The purpose of church is not to judge you, run you down, or tell you everything that's wrong with your life. Rather, a church will care for you with the love and compassion of Christ, share with you whatever grace and knowledge they have, and introduce you to the unsearchable riches of Christ. Our prayer is that God would work in your life so that you may come to understand your need for Him and the blessings available to you in Christ.

1

CHRISTIAN MORALS

What does it really mean to love God?

THE FIRST THING TO know about love is that the Bible sets God Himself forward as the ultimate example of what it means to love (1 John 4:8). This is one reason why love is so difficult to define: to understand love we must understand God! The best I can do is share the biblical passages that describe what love is. From these we can glean the elements of real love and work towards a definition that lines up with Scripture.

One clear element of love is that it involves self-sacrifice. John 3:16 and 1 John 3:16 tell us that the best example of love is Christ laying down his life for us. Christ, having everything and needing nothing, felt compassion for us and yielded His life. The only explanation we are given for this amazing gift is that He did it out of love. The Bible tells us that genuine love necessitates sacrifice. So then, if we truly love God, we will yield our lives as a sacrifice to Him just like Christ did for us (Romans 12:1; 2 Corinthians 5:14–15).

Closely related to this is the element of obedience. We do not often relate love and obedience in our culture, but the Bible states multiple times that love for God produces joyful obedience (Nehemiah 1:5; John 14:15; 15:10; 1 John 5:3).

Another element of love is that it produces certain qualities and virtues, as seen in 1 Corinthians 13:3–8. If we live in the love of God, we become more patient, kind, and considerate towards others.

So then, to love God means first to experience God's love for us. It then means to respond to His love with love (1 John 4:19), to respond to Christ's sacrifice with our own sacrifices (2 Corinthians 5:15), and finally to let God's love lead us into a lifestyle of obedience toward Him and loving service towards others.

What does the fear of the Lord mean?
Should I be afraid of God?

Let me explain the fear of the Lord with this illustration: I respect the rules of the road and would never deliberately drive on the wrong side, because I "fear" the consequences of a wreck. In the same way I am aware of the awesome power and magnitude of God and seek to live on the right side of His will. I do not tremble and shake while driving because I am confident of my own safety; so long as I follow the rules! In the same way I am not afraid of God as long as I have confessed my sins and seek to live in accordance with His will. I am assured of His good pleasure if I do so (1 John 1:9), and He is perfectly trustworthy and consistent.

The Bible tells us "The fear of the Lord is the beginning of wisdom." (Proverbs 1:7). Just like it defies common sense to ignore the laws for driving so it is ridiculous to ignore God's laws for living! The good news is if someone wakes up and realizes that they are on the wrong side of God they can quickly "course-correct" by asking forgiveness through Jesus Christ (John 3:16–18). Ultimately, we only need to be afraid of God if we scorn His offer of forgiveness and pardon, persisting in our sins rather than making peace through Christ (John 3:36).

If all I have to do to be saved is believe, what incentive is there for me to do good works?

You are correct that a person's salvation and eternal destiny are determined solely by our acceptance of the gospel of Jesus Christ; "Believe on the Lord Jesus Christ and you will be saved," (Acts 16:31). God does not hold our salvation over our heads, threatening to send us to hell if we don't fill a daily quota of good works (Romans 4:5; 5:1, 6, 8–9, etc.).

Does this mean that God doesn't care how we live? Is there no good reason to do good works? Absolutely not (Romans 6:15–23)! But the motive for good works must flow from a proper understanding of morality, not from fear of eternal destruction.

It is a self-evident truth that all life must be properly cultivated in order to flourish and be productive. What is true of plants and animals is true of people as well, only people possess spiritual, relational, and moral natures along with our physical bodies. Just as our physical lives are nourished by proper health choices; our spirit and relationships are nourished by proper moral choices, which can cause our lives to flourish. When we make wrong choices, we can destroy ourselves, our loved ones, and our potential to accomplish anything lasting or worthwhile in this world.

Let me give an example: two real people who made radically different moral choices. Their names are Abraham and Lot. While Abraham trusted God for his needs and chose generosity, his nephew Lot was selfish and grabbed the best for himself (Genesis 13:1–13). Lot trusted in the strength of man for safety, got captured, robbed, and nearly spent the rest of his life in bondage (Genesis 14:1–12). Abraham trusted God to preserve him from harm and accomplished bold and amazing feats through faith (Genesis 14:13–16). Lot chose to live among wicked men (Genesis 19:1–8; 2 Peter 2:7–8), compromised horribly (Genesis 19:7–9), and ended up penniless, broken, and homeless (Genesis 19:30–38). Abraham died in the bosom of his family at a ripe old age (Genesis 25:7–11), leaving a legacy of faith that has blessed and inspired countless believers for thousands of years (Hebrews 11:8–10). His family would produce such heroes as Joshua, King David, and the Lord Jesus Himself, all of whom were descended from Abraham and his son of faith, Isaac. While Lot kept his life and his salvation, he squandered God's blessings and accomplished nothing (1 Corinthians 3:14–15). Worse than that, his family was corrupted by the company that Lot chose to associate with. His legacy became tied to pagan nations (Genesis 19:36–38) and the power of God's promises went no farther. Lot died with no legacy, no accomplishments, and no future for his family. All things considered; wouldn't we rather be like Abraham?

Does God ever exercise judgment on Christians, or does his grace mean that we can live however we want to?

The grace of God means a great deal for Christians: forgiveness of sins, cleansing of impurity and a whole range of new blessings for life (Ephesians 1:3–14). God goes from being our judge to becoming our Father. This change in relationship means that we no longer need fear the eternal penalties for sin (John 10:28); we are forgiven in Christ (Colossians 2:13) and will not come into judgement (John 5:24).

However, it is *not* God's intention to let us to dive back into that sewer or leave us to do as we please. Again; God has become our Father, and misbehavior will bring chastening from Him (Hebrews 12:5–6). Take it from me, a heavenly spanking is not a pleasant experience.

This heavenly correction can take various forms, including an intensely guilty conscience (Psalm 32:3–5), physical sickness (1 Corinthians 11:30–32), loss of blessings and privileges (Revelation 2:5), and premature removal from the earth (Acts 5:1–5; 1 Corinthians 11:30). His parental punishment typically fits the crime and tends to place the Finger of God painfully and precisely upon the area of our lives He finds displeasing.

This doesn't mean we can judge others' suffering as evidence of God's displeasure. Bad things happen for a variety of reasons; not always because of a person's sin. Instead, we must each examine our own hearts to determine whether our suffering is merited or not. For myself, I typically know good and well when I've done something that God is not pleased with, and I don't have too much trouble knowing when I'm the recipient of His displeasure.

Now this may be daunting for many of us (and it should be), but we must remember that chastening for sin is another Christian privilege and a proof of our salvation (Hebrews 12:7–11) God only chastens His children, so if we find ourselves with a sensitive conscience and an inability to get away with sin, this shows us that our salvation is genuine and that God is protecting His beloved child from choices that He knows are harmful.

The Bible says we are saved in our spirit, doesn't that mean that God doesn't care what I do with my body?

Hmm, not so much! You see, there are two errors that we can make when it comes to God's perspective of our daily life. The first is to assume that God expects me to earn His favor by making right choices. This false perspective is corrected by verses such as Ephesians 2:8–9 and Romans 4:5, which clearly teach salvation by grace alone through faith alone. The opposite error is to assume that God doesn't care how we live, so long as we "believe in Jesus" or "pray a prayer." This perspective is also refuted by a myriad of Scriptures such as Ephesians 2:10, James 2:17, 1 Corinthians 6:19–20, Romans 12:1, and so on.

The whole counsel of Scripture reveals to us that we are saved by the grace of God *and* that He intends His grace to produce godly behavior in our daily lives. We are saved by a transforming faith (2 Corinthians 5:17, 21); and by a faith that works (James 2:26). The most obvious evidence of our saving faith is a changed lifestyle.

It is vital for us to understand that sin is not a set of demerits, nor is salvation a mere technicality to be stamped on our hand so we can go back to enjoying immoral life choices. Sin is cancer (Romans 7:24), it is the root cause of all misery in the human condition (Romans 1:18–32). Our sin is actively killing us and those we interact with (Romans 6:23). And because God cares about you,

He is actively seeking to deliver you from your sins so that you can begin to discover what the good life really is (John 10:10)! That is why the Bible warns us about sin, and that is why it instructs us to reject it, overcome it through faith in Christ, and be made whole and righteous in Christ.

The Bible says we ought to "turn the other cheek." Does this mean that Christians should not be soldiers or police officers? Is it always wrong to fight?

The Bible does instruct believers to turn the other cheek (Matthew 5:38–42). In context, the passage instructs us not to seek revenge for wrongs done against us personally, instead to show grace by repaying evil with good (see also Romans 12:18–20). Christians should let go of a vindictive spirit and forgive all offences committed against us.

However, this does *not* mean that all conflict or warfare is sinful. God gave humanity the responsibility of self-government and the right to back that government with force if necessary (Genesis 9:5–6). In other words, the human race is to hold itself to right behavior. Any extreme departure from right behavior (such as murder by an individual or rampant oppression by a nation) must be corrected; not in a spirit of vindictiveness, but out of faithfulness to God. This means that both police and soldiers, as instruments of good government, have the right to use force in defense of the helpless and to punish wrongdoing (Romans 13:1–4).

Police officers and soldiers are entirely deserving of our respect, praise, encouragement, and cooperation. They put their lives on the line to make the world a better place; performing an essential service to society by restraining the corrupting influence of sin and protecting those who cannot protect themselves. Our gratitude and prayers go out to all those who serve God and our country, both in the military and in law enforcement. God bless you!

With everything going on in the world today why aren't there more people going to church?

It might be a good idea to put this question to those who aren't coming! I for one would be very interested to hear the answers. I know many avoid church because they have never been taught the need for church. Others are turned off by hypocrisy or double standards. Still others may never have been invited or are nervous about going since they are not familiar with how church works. It is also possible for a church to disqualify itself from growth and ministry if its members are guilty of unfaithfulness or hypocrisy. Such a church will either be closed by God or die out naturally (Revelation 2:5). The Body of Christ must make sure that we are shining the light of Christ by living out our faith and loving our community. If we aren't being faithful then we have no right to complain that people aren't coming!

However, it is also important to understand that a church can be doing everything right and still experience long periods of fruitless labor. There are several reasons for this: one is that Satan is actively blinding the eyes of the world to prevent them from seeing the truth (2 Corinthians 4:3–5). As a church we can shine the light of Christ clearly (Matthew 5:16), but only God can open eyes that are blind so that they may respond to it (John 6:36–37, 44; 9:39). We must ask Him to do so. Another reason for delay is that God may be refining our character by teaching us perseverance. Most Christians are expected to develop the habit of consistent, godly behavior for a significant time *before* God begins blessing the work (James 1:2–4). Those who have faithfully aligned their lives with God's word are exhorted to continue doing so; it takes time for seeds planted to produce a harvest. So, in the words of Paul; "Let us not grow weary while doing good, for in due season we shall reap if we do not lose heart." (Galatians 6:9)!

Is America a Christian Nation?

I have read many works on the founding fathers and the birth of our nation, along with documents written by the founders during that period. The conclusion I have reached personally is that the Christian worldview was one of the principal influences on the founding fathers as they forged the framework of this country. I am as sure of the Christian basis for their decisions as I am about anything in secular history.

Let me give you an example of this influence; the founders based the structure of our government on the Christian doctrine of human depravity. Because they believed that no one is perfect they realized no one person can be trusted with absolute authority. This is why they vested power in a constitution rather than a monarch. It is also why they split the powers of government into three branches (taking a hint from Isaiah 33:22). They also devised checks and balances so that no one branch could take control.

Another example was the need they saw to teach future generations proper religious and moral truths so that they could function as moral citizens (Read the Northwest Ordinance, section 14, article 3; also, paragraph 27 of George Washington's farewell address). This desire to give future generations a sound religious, ethical, and practical foundation was the basis for their encouragement of education.

In short, the founding fathers based the laws of this nation on exceedingly noble and lofty ideals. Ideals taken largely from Christian thinkers of their day and drawn ultimately from the pages of Scripture. In the times and situations where our nation has lived up to those principles, we have seen a growth of peace, justice, and prosperity. In the times and situations where we have departed from those principles (such as the institution of slavery, mistreatment of Native Americans, and our present fascination with postmodern and atheistic philosophies) there has been a growth of dysfunction, injustice, and chaos. It is not so much about being a Christian nation; it is about governing according to truth, righteousness, and justice.

What's the point of getting baptized? What is it for?

Different churches and denominations will have different perspectives of the purpose of baptism, and most sincerely believe that their perspective is the one that most closely matches the perspective of Scripture. Part of the reason for this diversity is the range of Scriptures that pertain to the subject. When examined out of context, the different verses can seem to present contradictory views (compare 1 Corinthians 1:14–17 with Acts 2:38 for one example). While it is easy to focus on the verses that seem to match with what we've always been told, the trick is to identify ALL of the verses concerning baptism and come to understand the entire teaching of the Bible on the subject. The Christian that best accomplishes this will have the most biblical perspective of baptism.

My perspective is that baptism is a declaration of allegiance to Christ and the teachings of Christianity. While salvation from sins and new life in Christ are gained by placing our faith in Jesus Christ for forgiveness of sins (John 1:12; 5:24; Acts 16:29–31; etc.), baptism is a ceremony which pictures, demonstrates, and announces that saving faith to the church, family members, and friends (Acts 2:41). It can happen along with salvation, (in other words a person can choose to place their faith in Christ at the moment they are baptized), but typically the decision to be baptized will follow a person's decision to trust in Christ (Acts 8:35–38). The outward act of being ceremoniously immersed and raised out of the water symbolizes a person being spiritually crucified with Christ (Galatians 2:20; Romans 6:3), buried with Him in the grave (Romans 6:4), and raised to newness of life (Romans 6:4). It declares a commitment to live our lives as Christ would want us to (2 Corinthians 5:14–15), and can also set an example of faith for others to follow.

A person considering baptism should ask themselves several questions. First, "Do I genuinely believe that Jesus is my savior who died for my sins?" (Acts 8:36–37). "Have I accepted forgiveness and new life as a free gift from Him?" (Romans 4:5; Galatians 3:9). And finally; "Am I ready to follow Christ in my life and learn to act as a Christian should?" (2 Corinthians 5:17 & 21). If the answer to each of those questions is yes, then talk to your pastor about getting baptized!

Does the Bible mention anything about transgender people?

The most important verse to remember in regards to transgender people or anyone else is John 3:16. God has proven his love to the entire world by sending his Son to take the full penalty for our sins and offer us eternal life as a free gift. Other verses to consider are Psalm 16:11 and John 10:10, which tell us that God wants to bless us with abundant life. The guidelines for life we find in the Bible are designed to free us and enable us to live this blessed, abundant life.

With these truths in mind, we can examine what God tells us about our gender identity. Genesis 1:27 tells us that God designed the human race to consist of males and females. This lets us know that the gender we were born with was not a mistake; it is part of our Creator's good purpose (Psalm 139:13–14). Christians believe that genuine happiness in life is found by discovering God's 'acceptable and perfect will' for us (Romans 12:2). This means that we must take our identity from what God says about us, not what others tell us or what we invent about ourselves. We must learn to see our gender from God's point of view and trust Him to fulfil that reality in our lives. If we do this then we all can discover the happiness, identity, and acceptance that I believe many transgender people are seeking.

I feel guilty dumping all my aches and pains and troubles on my pastor. Should I keep them to myself or is it ok to share with the pastor?

The sensitivity of this question truly touches my heart. It is easy to thoughtlessly dump all of our cares upon others, whether pastors, family members, or friends. But the Bible calls us to consider one another, not just ourselves (Philippians 2:4). When we remember to be balanced and fair in our approach to emotional burdens, we bless everyone around us and preserve health and healthy relationships long-term.

A good pastor will be more than happy to come alongside you in a time of need. But if a pastor is always being handed other people's problems and has no one to come alongside of him, then he becomes the one in need! I know of many good, sincere pastors who have become less effective in ministry, jaded, and even bitter, because they are expected to fix everyone else's problems but received no support from their brothers and sisters in Christ themselves.

The key here is balance. All believers should be willing to come alongside others who are struggling and help them in time of need (Galatians 6:2). But each of us must also commit to carrying the loads we can; knowing that we all have problems and struggles; it is not right to overburden someone else so that you can have it easy (Galatians 6:3; 2 Corinthians 8:13–15).

I would suggest using the following questions to determine whether you are being considerate of your pastor in how you share emotional burdens. First, "Is this something that I can take care of myself?" If you've gotten into the habit of taking every little thing to your pastor, then there may be other solutions that you aren't taking advantage of, such as prayer. Second, "How is my pastor doing?" Does he seem tired? Stressed? Overburdened? You may find that your pastor needs your support even more than you need his! And finally, "If I'm going to ask my pastor to help with my emotional burden, is there a different need of his that I can help meet?" Even if your pastor is able to help bear your burden, there may be something else that you can do to bless him in return (Romans 1:12). A key to healthy relationships is a balance between giving and receiving. Relationships based upon mutual love and service are built to last and will bless a church for many years to come.

Should Christians go out and evangelize proactively or should we wait for opportunities to come to us?

Yes, and yes! The Bible lays out the great commission for His Church in Matthew 20:18–20, "Go, therefore and make disciples of all nations. . ." and also in Acts 1:8, "You shall be witnesses of me. . ." These verses make clear that our purpose for living as Christians is to share the gospel with the world and train up others to do likewise. The gospel (which literally means, "good news,") is the best news that has ever been shared with the world and it is vitally important for the world to hear it (John 3:18; John 5:24; etc.)! Now, this does not mean that every Christian is supposed to be a missionary or in full-time ministry, since Ephesians 4:11 says clearly that Christ intends "some to be apostles (i.e., missionaries or church planters) . . . some evangelists, etc." But it does mean that everyone saved by the grace of God ought to have a passion for sharing this good news with the world and we should be actively investing our time and money towards achieving that end.

However, there is also a place for what some call relational or reactive evangelism. Reactive evangelism consists of obeying the Bible's instructions regarding holy and godly living, thereby setting ourselves up as "the light of the world," (as seen in Matthew 5:14–16). When we live out the transformed life that God offers us through His Word, this demonstrates to the world that Jesus Christ really does change lives. This is attractive to those who are seeking and will cause them to approach us with questions. We are called to be ready to point them to Christ should such opportunities arise (1 Peter 3:15).

Let me offer a word of caution here, however. Because I know that many in our communities, both Christians and non-Christians, are sick of getting their arm twisted and lectured on church attendance or wrong living. Let me say clearly that I am sympathetic to those feelings and very concerned by them. There is a huge difference between biblical evangelism and arm twisting, and the key distinction is motivation. So-called evangelism with a motivation of legalism or moral obligation is blatantly false and misleads people about the true blessings of the gospel. Sincere evangelism is about joyfully inviting people we care about to share in the blessings of Christianity; it should leave people feeling drawn to Christ, not feeling pressured by Christians.

Why was the day of rest and meeting changed from Saturday to Sunday when the 4th commandment says to "Remember the Sabbath and keep it holy"?

When I was growing up, I would often try to overhear discussions between my mom and older brother if I heard her telling him to do something. If her instructions to my brother applied to me also, I wanted to be a step ahead in making sure I did what I needed to. But sometimes they discussed things that didn't apply to me, in which case I was off the hook.

It is important to remember that the Old Testament of the Bible was originally written to the "older brother" of the Christian Church: the Nation of Israel (also known as Jews, Israelites, children of Abraham, Isaac, and Jacob, and so on). When Christians read the Old Testament, we have to consider how (or even if) the instructions given to the Jews apply to our relationship with God today, since some do not carry over to Christianity. It's why we don't offer animal sacrifices to God (Hebrews 10:11–18), it's why we aren't bound by Old Testament Law (Galatians 3:10–13), and its why Christians shouldn't directly enforce Sabbath Rest (Acts 15:10–11).

The Law is still instructive to read and understand (Galatians 3:19; 1 Timothy 1:8), and the moral code that it upheld is the same morality that Christians live by today. That's why nine of the Ten Commandments are repeated in the New Testament as instructions for believers to live by today (see Ephesians 4:25, Ephesians 6:1–4 and 1 John 3:15 as examples).

The Sabbath law is the only command of the Ten Commandments that is not restated in the New Testament as a directive for Christians. We are not specifically told why but there are a few passages that offer insight. Hebrews 3:7—4:13 teaches that believers have a constant opportunity to enter God's rest through faith. Also, Jesus worked during His ministry to relax burdensome Sabbath restrictions that were self-defeating. He said "Sabbath was made for man; not man for the Sabbath." (Luke 6:1–5).

Many ministers and students of the word (myself included) still see periods of physical rest as important for health and well-being. Some will go so far as to recommend a regular weekly "sabbath" to rest and recharge. But some go too far by trying to tie Sunday meetings to the fourth commandment or force people to abide by Sabbath Law. The New Testament frequently warns against such teachings (Galatians 3:10–14; Colossians 2:16–17). In Christ we are free to enjoy God's rest however we choose, or even to deny ourselves rest and suffer the consequences! Sabbath law does not apply to Christians living today.

Is cancer a punishment from God?

I think it is best to approach the answer to this question through the framework of the gospel. The Bible tells us that God loved the world (i.e., all the people in the world) enough to send His beloved Son to die on our behalf (John 3:16). Jesus Christ, the Son of God, took the full punishment for our sins, bearing the brunt of God's wrath so that we could be healed (Isaiah 53:5). God is love (1 John 4:8), and that means everything that He does in our lives is done with our best interest at heart. Even bad things that happen to us can accomplish a good purpose (Romans 8:28).

The Bible gives us several reasons why bad things, like cancer, might happen, along with the ways that God can use it for good. Sometimes bad circumstances are simply a symptom of a broken world. You may have done nothing to deserve your situation, and there may be no discernable connection between what you are suffering and any choice that you have made (John 9:1–3). If that is the case then God's purpose is to work in your life to reveal His glory and nature (John 9:3); His will for you will become clear, in this life or the next. Trust in Him (Isaiah 40:31)!

Sometimes bad circumstances are the result of bad choices. Like the Prodigal Son we are blessed in life with freedom to choose (Luke 15:11–13). If we make poor or unwise choices then there are natural consequences for those choices, and we will eventually reap what we've sown (Luke 15:14–16; Galatians 6:7–8). This is not God's punishment; it is a wake-up call. Just like the horrible circumstances of the prodigal son caused him to seek forgiveness (Luke 15:17–24), so our difficulties remind us that God is waiting with open arms to receive us back if we will humble ourselves and turn to Him.

All this being said, the Bible does tell us that God is the judge of the Earth, the avenger of the weak and helpless, and the one who makes all things right (1 Chronicles 16:14; Psalm 58:10–11). But God is a merciful judge who withholds punishment until the last possible moment; hoping that we will repent (2 Peter 3:9). If you have done evil in your life, it is possible that your cancer is a punishment. If so, then God is still showing you mercy, because He has not killed you yet (Lamentations 3:22). He is giving you one last opportunity to repent of your sins and receive pardon and forgiveness (1 John 1:9). I would plead with you to take Him up on it!

As a pastor, what needs do you see in rural America?

When I consider the needs around us from a biblical worldview, the greatest need I see is for instruction in the truth. We, as a society, have forgotten the value of true morals and true religion. We've taken Bibles and the Ten Commandments out of our courtrooms. Prayer in schools is often frowned upon. Religious and moral instruction that used to be taken for granted is now almost completely absent from our culture.

Jesus Christ (teacher, savior, and the Son of God; the only man wiser than Solomon) said that truth can set us free (John 8:32). He also said in Luke 6:43–45 that good fruit can only come from good trees (which is quite self-evident). Thus, if we see ourselves surrounded by 'bad fruit' (i.e., evil works, destructive behavior, etc.), we must see that our problem is not primarily an environmental or economic problem, but a moral one.

How do we fix a moral problem? Jesus showed us how. He modeled the process of discipleship (life-to-life character training), shared the life-changing power of truth (Hebrews 4:12), and cooperated with the Holy Spirit to change lives of people around Him for the better (John 6:63). Through Christ and the Gospel, a work of transformation was sparked back then. And I believe God can accomplish the same thing and more in us, our neighbors, our communities (Titus 2:11–14)!

What would our communities look like if the following principles of morality were lived out more consistently in our lives: giving to the needy around us (Luke 6:30), loving our enemies (Matthew 5:43–44), overcoming evil with good (Romans 12:20–21), or loving our neighbor (Romans 13:10)? How would your neighbors respond if your life were filled to bursting with the Fruit of the Spirit (Galatians 5:22–23)? It takes time, prayer, intentional Bible study, God's cooperation, and consistent attendance at a God-fearing, Bible-teaching, Christ-reflecting church to instill these characteristics in ourselves and others. But twelve men, trained by Christ to boldly live out godly character, started a movement that changed the world. How many would it take to transform our communities? I'd like to find out!

Is there an unforgiveable sin? How can it be unforgivable if Christ died for all sin?

There are actually two situations where the Bible says that forgiveness is (or has been) withheld. The first situation is when we fail to forgive others, the second is the case of blasphemy against the Holy Spirit.

We can consider the case of unforgiveness by looking at two passages: the Lord's Prayer (Matthew 6:12, 14) and the Parable of the Unforgiving Steward (Matthew 18:22–35). These passages make God's expectation clear: He wants us to extend to others the same mercy that we received from Him. Severe discipline is promised to those who fail to do so (Matthew 18:34).

Of course, this raises some questions when we also consider passages that seem to promise unconditional and universal forgiveness for sin (John 5:24; Colossians 2:13; etc.). Don't worry! Reconciling these two ideas is quite simple when we examine the context of each passage more closely.

The first thing to notice is that all of the passages that declare to *non-Christians* how to obtain *eternal* forgiveness and go to heaven list faith as the one and only condition (John 3:16; Acts 16:12; Ephesians 2:8; etc.). The passages that say, "If you don't forgive others, God won't forgive you," are all addressed to disciples; people who have already trusted in Christ and seek to live in right relationship with Him. This causes many theologians to see God's promise of unforgiveness in the context of teaching and relationship, rather than a return to eternal damnation. In other words, refusing to forgive others does not counteract the effects of our salvation or nullify the promises of God. Instead, these promises concerning unforgiveness mean that God will treat a believer (in this life) just like they treat others. If we hold unforgiveness in our hearts our loving Father will correct us (Hebrews 12:6) by bringing the earthly consequences of our own sins back on our heads until we obey His command to forgive. Thus, the whole counsel of Scripture allows us to retain the comfort of God's eternal and unconditional salvation, while also heeding a necessary warning to avoid the sin of unforgiveness and forgive one another as we've been forgiven (Colossians 3:13).

Blasphemy against the Holy Spirit must be understood in the context in which it was written (Matthew 12:22–32; Mark 3:22–30). Matthew and Mark both record similar accounts of an interaction between Jesus and the Pharisees. Christ had performed a miracle that clearly demonstrated His divine nature. Rather than acknowledging His identity as the Son of God, the Pharisees attributed the miracle to Satan (a.k.a. Beelzebub). Jesus gave a rebuttal to their accusation (Matthew 12:25–29), then sternly warned the Pharisees that they had crossed a line by trying to twist an obvious work of the Holy Spirit into an act of the evil one (Matthew 12:31–32). He warned them that "speaking against the Holy Spirit" will not be forgiven (Matthew 12:32), and Mark made it very clear that Christ was referring specifically to their accusation of Him as being demon-possessed (Mark 3:29–30).

We must understand that the Holy Spirit was working with Christ through that miracle to present clear and convincing proofs of Christ's identity as the Son of God and promised Savior (John 10:24–25). Everyone confronted by those proofs had to make a choice: either to accept the obvious conclusion that Jesus is the Christ and believe in Him, or to deny reality and make up an excuse that would allow them to live as they pleased. The Pharisees chose to believe the absurdity that Satan was casting himself out rather than accept that Jesus was the Son of God. They committed the sin of unbelief, which in this passage is called blasphemy against the Holy Spirit. And since belief is the one requirement for forgiveness (John 5:24), unbelief is the one sin not covered by the cross. Failure to believe clear proofs about Jesus is the only truly unforgivable sin; it is the only thing that can keep us from going to Heaven (John 3:18).

Does a person have to go to church to be saved?

There are multiple scriptures throughout the Bible that tell us that there is only one requirement for receiving forgiveness of sins and everlasting life as a free gift; believing in Jesus Christ. (John 3:18; Acts 16:30–31; Romans 4:5; Eph. 2:8–9).

That being said, salvation is more than a 'get-out-of-hell-free' card, it is a life-changing experience that serves as the beginning of a whole new life. If we have genuinely placed our faith in Christ, we should have a desire to get baptized, spend time around other believers, learn more about God and the Gospel, worship Him, and tell others about Him. Attending a good, Bible-teaching church is the easiest way to accomplish these things! In fact, these actions follow salvation so naturally that they are sometimes included in Gospel invitations (Mark 16:16; Acts 2:38; James 2:26)!

In short you do not need to attend church, be baptized, or do good works to *become* a Christian or have eternal life (John 5:34; also think of the thief on the cross in Luke 23:39–43). However, these actions are vital parts of *being* a Christian! If you have placed your faith in Christ, I strongly encourage you to be baptized and become involved with a solid Bible-teaching church!

If you tithe are you more apt to go to heaven?

Bible verses such as Habakkuk 2:4, John 3:36, Romans 4:5, Romans 6:23, Romans 11:6, and Galatians 2:21 (to name just a few) all make it very clear that eternal life in heaven is offered by God to all as a *completely* free gift. there is nothing we must do to qualify for this gift and indeed nothing we could do to earn it even if we wanted to (Isaiah 64:6). All we have to do is accept eternal life as a gift from God by trusting in Jesus.

Giving money to God, church, or charity earns you no merit with God at all (Luke 18:9–14). In fact, He finds any attempt to gain merit from good works positively repulsive (Isaiah 64:6; Romans 3:20; Galatians 3:1–3). God loves a cheerful giver (2 Corinthians 9:7), and He finds great joy in those who reflect His gracious character by giving freely just as they have freely received (Matthew 10:8; 2 Corinthians 9:6–8).

To conclude: showing free, God-like generosity to God's work, His church, or the needy does not make it more likely to *go* to heaven, it shows that you are *becoming* a child of heaven by living as God lives and giving as He gives.

2

CHRISTIAN LIVING

Isn't it judgmental to disapprove of someone's lifestyle?

PROPERLY RESPONDING TO THE sins of other people is a delicate balancing act, particularly in today's atmosphere of hypersensitivity. While Christians are sometimes required to share the truth about sin with others, the sins that we ought to be the most aware of and concerned about are our own (1 Timothy 1:15)! If we are going to avoid the pitfalls of hypocrisy, condemnation, and self-righteousness we must examine ourselves carefully in three areas.

First, we must have a right perspective of ethics, which we draw from the pages of Scripture. I cannot accurately diagnose another person's heart if I cannot tell right from wrong. A twisted moral compass will misdirect me and anyone that I address about sin.

Secondly, we must have hearts that are free from sin ourselves. An oft-forgotten effect of sin is that it blinds us to our own guilt while making us hypersensitive to the guilt of others. This makes hypocrisy distressingly easy for believers and unbelievers alike, and it is why Christ instructs us to take the log out of our own eye before we try to take the speck from our brother's (Matthew 7:5).

We must learn that awareness of other's sin is a reminder to check our own hearts.

The third thing we must check ourselves for is a proper attitude towards the sinner. During His earthly ministry, Jesus had many occasions to interact with sin. While He saw all sin perfectly and addressed it frequently, His response was most often made within a context of love and compassion. If we do not experience the same sorrow, pity, and compassion that Christ felt towards sinners, then we have a wrong perspective and must confess that and repent before God. While we must be on guard against the sins of unrighteousness (lying, stealing, sexual sins, etc.), we must also resist the temptations of self-righteousness (hypocrisy, condemnation, and pride).

What does the Bible have to say about anger? Is it a sin to be angry?

The Christian's ultimate standard for right and wrong is the character of God Himself (see Matthew 5:48 for one example). This gives us a solid basis for saying that it is not always sinful to be angry, since we are given many examples of both God and Jesus Christ becoming angry (Matthew 21:12–17; Romans 1:18). That being said, anger can lead to sin even though it isn't always wrong to be angry. Therefore, it must be handled carefully.

A good place to start is with the question, "Is it right for me to be angry?" (Jonah 4:4). Anger is a natural response to a seemingly unfair situation. However, we must test our perspective against God's word to know whether anger is the proper response (hint; hitting your thumb with a hammer is not a good reason). If our anger is not justified, we must let it go. If it is justified, we move to the next passage.

Ephesians 4:26 tells us not to sin when we are angry. Even justified anger can tempt us to lash out in temper or outbursts of wrath. We must exercise self-control; instead of lashing out in sin we must restrain any wrong responses and make sure that we are responding to the situation rightly.

One final passage (1 Peter 2:23–25) uses Jesus Christ as the ultimate example of self-control to show us how to lay our anger to rest. Just before His crucifixion Jesus was subjected to the cruelest provocations imaginable. He was slapped in the face. He was spit upon. The soldiers blindfolded him then hit him repeatedly. Despite all of this Jesus kept his cool and 1 Peter 2:23 tells us how He did it; "He entrusted Himself to the One who judges justly." The way that we allow anger and wrath to pass away from us is by entrusting the situation to our Heavenly Father through prayer, knowing that he will handle the situation with perfect justice, skill, and timing.

Where in the Bible does it talk about how to be more patient?

Let me approach the topic of patience by beginning with its opposites: impatience and frustration. We often approach life with an expectation of how things ought to be. When these expectations are not met, we can become frustrated and impatient. Instead of adjusting our expectations to better fit with reality, we try harder to make reality line up with our expectations. And we all know how well that goes! This is the root cause of impatience.

The good news is that there are a few basic Bible truths that can help us correct wrong perspectives, avoid frustration, and live with greater patience. The first truth is that we live in a fallen world; therefore, nothing is going to go perfectly (Ecclesiastes 1:13–15). While we cannot foresee every problem, it really shouldn't surprise us that a broken world doesn't always function like it should. If we accept this reality and are willing to roll with setbacks and hardships it can help us keep our blood pressure in check. A wise person expects the unexpected and writes all their plans in pencil.

A second helpful truth is that believers in Christ are going to live forever. God calls us as His children to remember that the hardships of this world are temporary (2 Corinthians 4:16–17; 1 John 2:15–17). While frustration focuses us on the present; we must learn to counter that pattern by remaining mindful of eternity. So, if you begin to feel frustrated, stop and ask yourself, "will this matter in 20 years?"

Finally, we must understand that our life and all our earthly possessions are on loan from God, and we must give them back one day (Job 1:21). Sometimes God takes away things that we couldn't keep anyway so that He can give us godly character which we will keep forever (Romans 5:3–4). Remembering this helps us appreciate situations that test our patience and helps us wait upon God to complete His perfect work (James 1:2–4).

Does the Bible have anything to say about raising children?

The Bible does indeed have a vast amount of valuable teaching on the subject of raising children. The family was designed by God (Genesis 1:27), and He has given instructions to guide us in every aspect of it. In fact, there is so much information in the Bible on this subject I couldn't possibly fit it all in one article! Specific questions pertaining to raising children would allow me to share in greater detail. For now, I can cover some basics.

At its core, the raising of children is about exploring the mysterious relationships within the Godhead itself. When God created men and women in His image (Genesis 1:27), He created them with the ability to beget children (Genesis 1:28), because He exists eternally as Father, Son, and Holy Spirit. The Father exercises supreme authority (Psalm 103:19) and displays His perfect love for the Son (John 5:20). The Son willingly and joyfully expresses obedience and submission to the Father (John 4:31–34; Philippians 2:5–8; etc.), and the Spirit joins in the work of the Father and the Son. All Three working all things in perfect harmony, unison, and joy.

In order to introduce us to this joyful unity, God blesses parents with children. We are given the tremendous privilege and sobering responsibility of caring for the most precious piece of God's creation: a human soul bearing the Image of God. As parents we are to emulate the love and authority of the Father (Ephesians 6:4), our children are meant to demonstrate the loving fulfillment of obedience (Ephesians 6:1–3). Parents are given the authority they need to care for and train the children they are given (Exodus 20:12).

Raising the children entrusted to us by God is always considered a special privilege and blessing in Scripture (Psalm 127:4–5). And while the presence of sin in both parents and children has destroyed the full experience of this blessing (Romans 1:28–30; 2 Timothy 3:1–2; etc.), the grace available to us through Christ can help redeem our families and move us back towards God's original purpose (1 Peter 1:3).

As a parent with grown children, I'm struggling to know how involved in their decisions I should be. What does the Bible say?

This is a great question. The Bible reveals a very important change that should take place in our relationship with our children when they are grown. If we are not intentional in making this change at the proper time, we can cause a lot of hardship for ourselves and our children.

First, we should note the *un*changing basis for parent-child relationships in Exodus 20:12. The fourth commandment tells us all, adults and children, to honor our father and mother. Parents are always entitled to respectful treatment, because God says so!

Another passage instructs children to obey their parents in the Lord (Ephesians 6:1). The primary way in which children honor their parents is by joyfully and willingly obeying their instructions. Parents are right to uphold and require obedience from their young children. And they are right to exercise authority over the choices their children make.

However, there comes a point when children step out from under their parents' authority, either to become independent adults or to join with a spouse in founding a new family unit with a new authority structure. This is seen most clearly in Genesis 2:24.

The perspective of this student of Scripture (along with many Bible teachers) that the point at which this takes place is the point of financial independence. As long as my children are dependent upon me it is right for them to submit to my authority. The responsibility of providing for them is balanced by the right and privilege of authority over them. To separate from one is to separate from both.

So then, if your children have left home and established financial independence from you, then your relationship is no longer one that contains any direct authority. It is still right for them to honor your sacrifices, greater experience, and greater wisdom. And hopefully your relationship with them is healthy enough that they feel comfortable seeking your advice and counsel as needed. However, we must no longer require obedience from them, because God has instructed them to separate from that. Their life is now their own and we must give them freedom to make their own choices, even wrong choices, and learn from their mistakes.

I know the Bible says I'm supposed to let go of anger and bitterness. But I can't seem to do that. Does Scripture ever specifically tell us *how* to let go of anger and bitterness?

That is an important element, isn't it? The commands and instructions of Scripture are often easier to make out than the process for doing so. But the process is there, and careful sifting can draw it out.

To start, let's set some definitions. Anger is our natural, emotional response to perceived injustice. It alerts us when life doesn't seem fair, so that the injustice can be resolved. It's not wrong to feel anger but we must process it quickly and properly so that it doesn't lead to sin or turn sour (Ephesians 4:26–27).

If anger is allowed to settle into our heart it can turn into bitterness. Bitterness is a very caustic emotion; it eats into our soul, doing far more damage to us then the person we're bitter with. Bitterness is an emotional wound that MUST be cleansed and healed (Hebrews 12:15).

Now to the how. If anger and bitterness are caused by a lack of justice then the solution is to identify the situation that made us angry and resolve the injustice itself. This is the major sticking point of anger and bitterness; if we feel unable to resolve an unjust situation, anger remains. But God has given us the power to resolve injustice, so that we don't have to remain deadlocked (Romans 12:19; 1 Peter 2:23).

Some human means for resolving injustice include: personal discussion and appeal (Matthew 18:15), mediation (Matthew 18:16–17; 1 Corinthians 6:1–5), and government (Romans 13:3–4). However, if these corrective measures fail to provide us with justice and resolution, we can still entrust the situation to God and forgive the offender, because, eventually, He will make all things right (Genesis 18:25).

Resolving the wrong done by any of the means listed above resolves our feelings of anger and bitterness and replaces them with peace and rest. This is what it means to "Let all bitterness, wrath, anger, and clamor be put away from you," (Ephesians 4:31). A pastor, biblical counselor, or other mature Christian may sometimes be needed to help us walk through this process.

Is it a sin to drink alcohol/get drunk?

One way that sin is described in the Bible is "trespass" or "transgression." Both terms mean to go beyond the boundaries of acceptable behavior; to step into forbidden or harmful territory. You see, the Bible has laid out guidelines that teach us beneficial and upright behavior. Christians are completely free to enjoy all of God's blessings within these boundaries. But when we seek things which are outside of God's will, the bomb starts ticking and problems begin to accumulate.

Alcohol and the process of fermentation are some of God's many created blessings, and they have many benefits. One is the fact that alcohol sterilizes and kills bacteria, which made it hugely beneficial in the ancient world (Luke 10:34), before other reliable means of water purification had been discovered. This is why (3/4 watered down) wine was the most common and healthiest beverage in Jesus' day (Luke 5:37–39; John 2:3 etc.). In fact, Paul recommends it to Timothy as a stomach remedy (1 Timothy 5:23). So then, those who follow the example of Christ, Paul, and Timothy by responsibly consuming alcohol may do so without qualms.

However, a cardinal virtue of Scripture is self-control (1 Corinthians 6:12; Galatians 5:23). If a person consumes alcohol to the point that they are controlled by the drink, then they have gone too far (Galatians 5:19, 21; Ephesians 5:18). They are drunk, and there are many hazards and consequences that accompany that state. It is NOT healthy and can easily lead to harm. Drunkenness is repeatedly condemned in Scripture and all of God's people are called to remain sober and temperate (i.e., self-controlled; Luke 21:34; Romans 13:13; 1 Timothy 3:8; 1 Peter 4:3; etc.).

One more point that should be mentioned is that Scripture encourages Christians to be led by their conscience in questionable areas (Romans 14:14, 23). If a person is not comfortable consuming alcohol at all, either because of their upbringing or because of past struggles with alcoholism, then they should avoid it. But they should not consider themselves more "spiritual" or try to impose that standard upon others (Romans 14:2–4).

How do I know if I'm sinning or not? Is there a list of sins that I can look at?

If I were speaking to this person face to face, I would ask them why they want to know if they are sinning or not. If they are thinking that they need to fill out a checklist of righteous behavior in order to avoid being punished or earn God's favor, then it's important to know that God doesn't work like that. He has forgiven believers all trespasses in Christ (Col. 2:14) and we will not come into judgement for sinning or breaking God's rules (John 5:24; 1 Jn. 3:9). Our blessings depend upon our faith and Christ's Righteousness, not our good works (Ro. 5:4).

It is not healthy for a believer to become too focused upon rules or lists of sin (Ro. 10:4; Gal. 3:10; Col. 2:20–23). Just like focusing on a ditch while driving can cause us to drive into it if we're not careful, so focusing upon how we aren't supposed to live can strengthen temptation. Christians should focus upon our righteous opportunities and blessings in Christ (Ro. 8:5 Col. 3:1–2).

Only after saying this will I offer an answer to this question. Just as an awareness of the white lines on a road can keep us from crossing them, so an awareness (not a focus) of the lines we shouldn't cross as Christians can be helpful to check that we are still moving in the right direction. With that in mind, passages like Romans 12:1–21 and Ephesians 4:25–32 are both helpful passages to check ourselves against

Is it sinful to have doubts or questions about God? If so, how can I get rid of them?

It is not sinful to have doubts or questions about God. There are far too many examples in Scripture of godly believers expressing doubts and struggles with God and other mature believers to think that. Some examples include a man named Asaph who felt that God was being unfair in allowing evil people to prosper (Ps. 73), as well as the prophet Habakkuk who decided that he was going to sit on a watchtower until God answered his questions about evil (Habakkuk 2:1). We can also see from Christ's life that he welcomed questions and gave truth to those who sought it (see Matthew 18:21–22; John 14:5–6, 22–23 for just a few examples).

God is perfectly aware that our imperfect knowledge of Him will sometimes cause us to face situations or problems that we find confusing or a struggle (Ps. 103:11, 13). He has provided us with several tools to help resolve our doubts and questions. Namely: the Holy Spirit (John 16:13), the Bible (Ps. 119:105), and pastors and teachers in the Church (Eph. 4:11–12).

However, I would like to offer the following guidelines when it comes to seeking the answers to our doubts or questions. First, we must remember that an infinite God is not accountable to finite man (Isaiah 55:8–9; Habakkuk 2:1). We cannot hold God to our wrong standards or demand that He conform to our worldly perspectives. We must also remember to be both patient and persistent when pursuing truth since we may not find an answer right away. Sometimes God's people have to wait years to discover answers to our questions. There are some questions that won't be answered this side of heaven. The question we must ask ourselves is, "Has God answered enough of my questions for me to give him the benefit of the doubt on things I don't yet understand?

I'm having a hard time forgiving someone in my life; is there anything in the Bible that can help me?

The word forgiveness in the Bible is a financial term that refers to the cancellation of a debt. If you sin against someone else, the Bible says that you incur a debt to God, society, and the victim of that sin. But forgiveness strikes out that obligation and releases all rights to be repaid for the wrong done. This does not mean that we cannot feel hurt or upset by sin, it does mean that we can no longer seek payback or reparations.

So much for the definition, now how do we do this? If we are struggling to forgive others in our life the best thing to do is to put their sin in perspective by comparing the large debt we have incurred towards God with the (relatively) minor debt incurred by the person who sinned against us. In Matthew 18:20–32 Jesus walked his disciples through this idea. He told Peter that, even though sin does cause a legitimate grievance (since all human beings have a fundamental right to be treated fairly), we ought to lay down our right to payback because of the even greater offence that we have all incurred before God. All sin is an eternal offense to the God of Heaven and the just punishment for that sin is eternal separation from Him in hell. Despite God's legitimate grievance against us, He chose to show us mercy, compassion, and forgiveness by sending His Son to pay our debt for us. In the light of God's amazing forgiveness of our eternal debt, He asks us to forgive others' earthly trespasses. Jesus also explains in no uncertain terms that God is not happy with anyone who accepts mercy and forgiveness for himself while unmercifully withholding forgiveness from others (Mt. 18:31–35)! The basic argument of this passage and others (Ephesians 4:32; Colossians 3:13) is that Christians simply cannot afford to withhold forgiveness from others; we need it too much ourselves!

I have a dear relative who doesn't believe in God, what can I do to help them?

Prayer is always a good option when concerned for those we care about (Philippians 4:6–7). Beyond that, each situation is unique and I hesitate to offer much in the way of direct advice. However, I would offer the following thoughts from Scripture and invite you to consider how they apply to your situation.

First, has your loved one heard the gospel message (Romans 10:14)? The Bible tells us that there is only one way to receive forgiveness and eternal life, and that is through Christ (John 14:6; Acts 4:12). It can be uncomfortable to share your faith with another, but your concern for their well-being and relationship with them puts you in the best position to share that truth with them. Tell them how you came to believe in Christ, and share from your heart.

Remember, all we can do for others is explain the way of salvation, we cannot force them to believe (Acts 26:28–29; 2 Corinthians 4:2). Even if they do not accept it right away it doesn't mean you are a failure or did it wrong. You're now able to move to the next step: being a witness in how you live.

Once people know where you stand, they will begin watching your life to see if the truth has made any difference how you live (1 Peter 3:15–16). This is why Christians are called to live a blameless and upright life (Philippians 2:14–15) that demonstrates faith in Christ to the world. They should be able to see the light of Christ in our lives (Matthew 5:16), which will also be evidence for them of the life-changing power of the gospel (2 Corinthians 5:17).

We can all improve in each of these areas, and if the salvation of the lost depended solely on us they'd be in a sad way. Which is why the last and most important thing to remember is to continually entrust the situation to God through prayer (Col. 4:3; 1 Timothy 2:1, 4). Remember that salvation is God's work, and He is able to reach even the most hard-hearted (1 Timothy 1:13–16). Pray earnestly for your loved one and never give up on them; trust that God will do what is best in their lives (Proverbs 3:5–6).

I am concerned about my kids getting mixed up in drugs and alcohol. Does the Bible offer any advice on how to keep them from it?

Proverbs is one of the best books of the Bible to go to for warnings about abusing alcohol and other substances, and most of it is already presented in the framework of parental advice (Proverbs 20:1; 23:29–35; 31:4–6). While Biblical warnings against drunkenness and carousing are well known, these verses also set out the manner in which the advice is offered. The methods and expressions used in Scripture can guide our approach to the subject as well.

One common approach is to inform our children of the ultimate consequences for intemperance (Proverbs 23:29–35). It is easy for children to see the fun of partying, being popular, and getting drunk. But they must be shown the end result: the poverty, disorders, and dysfunction which drunkenness can so easily lead to. While we must not be judgmental or condemning of those trapped in sin, we should connect the dots for our children in age-appropriate ways so that they understand the danger that drunkenness poses for them.

Another helpful point is the use of affirmation. Our children are being bombarded by commercials and other cultural influences that present alcohol as harmless, cool, and positive. As parents, it is essential for us to affirm our children in doing what is right. We must help them see that the way to get lasting acceptance and well-being is through making right choices (Proverbs 1:8–9; 3:13–18).

Proverbs 31 may be especially helpful if your child is already heading down that road; it contains an impressive tongue-lashing from a mother who caught her son partying with alcohol and loose women. Notice that she allows her son to see her genuine shock and concern (v. 1), she tells him that he has been given too much to let alcohol waste his life (v. 4), reminds him of the peril of what he is doing (vv. 5–6), and calls him to set his focus on doing what is right and making a difference with his life (vv. 8–9). These words are shared out of genuine love and concern, and they helped turn this young king from a profligate wastrel into a wise ruler (Proverbs 25:11).

Simply cutting these verses out of the Bible and throwing them at our children is *not* going to effectively dissuade them from wrong choices. *We* must study these verses (as well as examples from real life) and learn from them what will happen to our children if they go down that road. When these truths sink into our hearts, they generate genuine feelings of concern for our children's well-being, which will show up in all our conversations with them on the subject. That emotion, lovingly communicated (1 Corinthians 13:1), will teach them the genuine danger behind the reckless use of drugs and alcohol more than any speech ever could. While we all have been given freedom by God to make our own choices in life, learning and modelling biblical character can provide a strong influence towards right living to our children.

I'm worried that one day I will lose my faith; how can I make sure that I don't fall away?

There is an ongoing theological debate on how and if the warnings against falling away relate to a believer's salvation. I am not going to go into that because I don't think that's the focus of this question. Regardless of the details and implications, the Bible does repeatedly warn believers of the danger of falling away. This is seen particularly in the book of Hebrews; which was written for this very purpose (see Hebrews 2:12; 10:39, etc.). And from the book of Hebrews, we can draw principles on how to remain true.

The first is to keep our heart soft and obedient towards God (Hebrews 3:7–8). God is at work in our lives removing sin and leading us in righteousness. We are called to submit to this work even though it can be difficult and painful. If we reject God's leading once it will be more difficult to hear his voice in the future (cf. 1

Thessalonians 5:19). This can cause us to fade away from the faith over time.

Another danger is failing to grow in our understanding of the Word. Christians are meant to progress from spiritual immaturity towards full knowledge of God and His Word (Hebrews 5:12—6:3). Failing to do so can lead to a lack of responsiveness to the Word (i.e., dullness of hearing; Hebrews 5:11) and a general spiritual 'sluggishness' (Hebrews 6:12). We are told plainly that this failure to grow in the word leads directly to falling away (Hebrews 6:4–6; but read v. 9 for reassurance!).

When our commitment to Christ is challenged by difficult circumstances, we will have need of endurance (Hebrews 10:36), We must understand that enduring difficult trials is part of being a Christian (2 Timothy 2:3), and trust that God will not allow us to be overcome or destroyed (cf. 1 Corinthians 10:13). Once His refining work is completed the reward will be more than worth the cost (Hebrews 10:35; 11:6).

One more guideline we are given is to persist in Christian fellowship (Hebrews 10:24–25). Because the gospel is so important and the stakes of faithful living so high, we are exhorted to gather regularly with fellow believers so that we may encourage and exhort each other to keep the faith. Failing to meet regularly with like-minded, committed Christians will also lead to spiritual lethargy. We must not forsake the fellowship!

The danger of falling away is presented as a legitimate concern in many places in the New Testament. However, if we are striving for faithfulness and following the Bible's guidelines, confessing our sins, and remaining close to God, we can trust in His guidance to preserve us and keep us until He calls us home.

What are some ways that I can be living out God's will for my life right now?

I am excited by this question! The decision to begin living out God's will for us is second only to the decision to trust Christ as Savior and Lord! God's will for us is known through His Word; the

Bible and there are several passages that can help a person begin living out His will today!

The first helpful verse is 2 Peter 2:2. This verse tells us to desire the Word of God like a newborn desires milk. Since I have a baby in the house right now this illustration hits home! Like milk to a newborn baby the Bible is a necessity for believers, but it's an acquired taste. It takes discipline to develop the habit, but that habit is one of the most important things for believers to have! Get into the Word! Joining a Bible Study or Sunday School can help us with this.

The next step is to let God's word begin shaping our character by living out what it teaches (1 Thessalonians 4:3; James 1:21–25). Christians are called to grow in righteous character so that others can see the transforming power of the gospel. Within a few years of becoming a Christian, we ought to have grown up enough to understand God's word for ourselves, know the process for overcoming sin, and begin taking on responsibilities within the family of God

Stepping into a role of service in a local church is a final big step for a believer seeking God's will. God wants all believers to be a part of a local family or body of believers (1 Corinthians 12:12–13). Each Christian is given unique gifts by God partly so that they may exercise those gifts to benefit other believers (1 Peter 4:10–11). You don't have to have an official title or anything, just think about the things you're good at (fixing things, teaching kids, etc.) and think of creative ways to use those gifts to bless the church.

Why are we supposed to go to church? What is church good for?

The word translated "church" in our Bibles refers to a 'called-out assembly." In other words, a church is a group of people who have been called out of their culture and society by God to become part of something completely new and different (1 Peter 2:9–10). Members of this group are called saints (Colossians 1:2), beloved brethren chosen by God (1 Thessalonians 1:4), holy brethren (1 Thessalonians 5:27), believers in Christ (Acts 4:32; 5:14), and the body of Christ (Romans 12:5). Christians are special; set apart by God for His unique work through the gospel.

Because of a Christian's new nature, it is necessary for him or her to have a time to gather together with other, like-minded believers for encouragement, fellowship, and teaching. 'Birds of a feather flock together,' as the saying goes! Times of genuine Christian fellowship are blessed occasions for prayer, sharing, fellowship, encouragement, and learning (Acts 2:42–45). Paul, in 1 Corinthians 12:12–26, elaborates upon the similarities between a local church and a physical body. Just as each part of the body performs a special task for the body, while also relying on other parts as much as they rely upon it; so it is with a healthy group of Christians.

It is tragically common for people (including pastors) to see church as a religious obligation or social duty. Church becomes defined as a building or a weekly meeting instead of the 'called-out assembly' that it truly is. This can change what ought to be a joyful fellowship into a monotonous drudgery of social obligation. Yet I think the earliest followers of Jesus would have been surprised to find it this way. The perspective we find in the Bible is that gathering together in church is as necessary for Christians as an attachment to a body is necessary for a hand!

3

DEATH AND WHAT COMES AFTER

Is it possible that hell is just a reference to the struggles of this life?

BELIEVERS MUST CONSTANTLY BE on guard against the urge to shy away from truths that make us uncomfortable. It is very tempting to explain away the Bible passages which discuss hell and eternal torment, and there are a variety of ways that people have attempted it. The problem is that all of these attempts are the theological equivalent of sticking our heads in the sand.

It really must come back to the simple message of Scripture. In order to benefit from the profound promise of John 3:16, I must take the verse at face value and accept the truths which it clearly communicates. Many find this easy to do because the truths of John 3:16 are fairly pleasant to believe in. But if we are to be honest and consistent in our understanding of God's Truth then we must be just as straightforward in interpreting verses such as Luke 16:23–24, Revelation 20:10, and Revelation 21:8. Each of these verses indicate that the final destination for the ungodly is a place of profound and eternal torment. The only escape from this eternal doom is faith in Christ's atoning sacrifice (John 3:18, 36).

God tells us these truths with good reason. He does not desire any to perish but all to come to repentance (2 Peter 3:9). The passages that teach about hell are a warning to people everywhere to escape the wrath of God through the outlet He has provided: faith in Christ. But how can people respond to these warnings unless they are clearly communicated (Romans 10:14)? As uncomfortable as it is, Christians must remain committed to the clear truths of Scripture; we must clearly communicate the *bad* news of eternal peril so that people can understand the *good* news of deliverance through Christ!

Does God decide who goes to heaven and who goes to hell?

While I do not claim to have all of the answers when it comes to God's sovereign will and our own responsibility, there are certain truths from Scripture that I can state with confidence.

First, Christ died for the sins of the world and provides everyone with the opportunity to go to heaven (John 3:16). While God knows who will accept this gift and who will not, this does not prevent Him from showing truly unconditional love by offering salvation to all; even those who will reject Him. This is seen in many verses (John 3:15–18; Ro. 5:6–8; etc.), but most clearly in 1 Timothy 4:10 where God is called, "The Savior of *all* men, especially those who believe." This does not mean that everyone will go to heaven (John 3:18); it means that God's offer of salvation is offered to all in good faith, but effective only for those who believe.

Second, we are told that God desires everyone to go to heaven. 1 Timothy 2:4 says that God "desires all men to be saved," and 2 Peter 3:9 says that God is "not willing that any should perish." This desire will not be completely fulfilled since we know that many will not believe in Christ but it shows us God's heart and that other factors can keep Him from receiving all His desires. In other words, we are not mindlessly carrying out God's program; we have influence on our existence and our eternity.

The Bible does talk about God "choosing" people to fulfill certain roles in His divine will (Ro. 9:10–13; Gal. 1:15–16). These sovereign choices (sometimes referred to as God's election) are primarily concerned with God's call upon a person's life, and while this has implications for salvation, that is not the focus. In short, God does not choose certain people to go to heaven and others to go to hell. He sovereignly reveals His grace and nature to certain people and assigns them positions as a part of His mysterious will.

If someone hasn't heard what the Bible says about what it takes to be saved, how can that be their fault? Will they go to heaven anyway?

Before we can understand the answer to this question, I have to lay some groundwork about God, His rules, and our fallen nature. We must begin with the fact that God is our Sovereign Creator (Genesis 1:1; Psalm 100:3). Since God made us, He has the right to make rules to govern our lives. He also has the right to decide the consequences for breaking the rules. His rules have a very basic foundation: those who do good are rewarded and those who do evil are punished (Romans 2:6–8). The problem is; nobody kept the rules (Romans 3:10–12). Because every single human being has violated God's standard, He would have been perfectly justified to punish us all with death. However, He chose to offer the world a way of escape through faith in Jesus Christ. Whoever believes in Him receives forgiveness and eternal life as a free gift (John 3:16; Romans 6:23).

Everyone who has ever lived has been surrounded with evidence for God's existence (Psalm 19:1; Romans 1:20). The evidence we see around us in creation should have been enough to convince us to begin looking for an omnipotent creator. The fact that it doesn't demonstrates our fallen nature and the fact that we are deserving of judgment. Therefore, those who do not respond to God's offer of pardon are deserving of judgment, whether they reject the grace of God as revealed in creation or His grace revealed in the gospel (John 3:18, 36; Romans 3:11–12). As one person put it: "Humanity deliberately dove into the floodwaters of sin. The question we should ask is not "why doesn't God pull everyone out?" it is: "why did God pull anybody out?

Knowing my days are numbered, where in the Bible can I find comfort and the courage to accept my death?

Probably one of the best passages for overcoming the fear of death is 1 Corinthians 15:20–58 (especially vv. 50–58), which describes Christ's victory over death and the grave on behalf of those who believe. I especially like verses 54–57 that describe death as a defeated enemy and a conquered foe. Death is rightly terrifying for many (Luke 16:19–31), but believers in Christ can rest in the promise that Jesus Christ has defeated death for us (Hebrews 2:14–15; Revelation 20:6). Death for Christians is like a savage dog that has had all its teeth removed; it can't hurt us anymore!

Another thing that can make us uncomfortable with the thought of dying is the fear of the unknown. But God has provided for this as well, informing us what happens to us when we die. First, Christians are told that the moment we lay down our mortal flesh we are present with the Lord (2 Corinthians 5:6–8). We are also told that we lay down our mortal body merely to exchange it for a new, glorified, spiritual body (1 Corinthians 15:42–43; 2 Corinthians 5:1–5) and that Christ has prepared for us a dwelling place so that we may be with Him always (John 14:1–3, 18). Not only that, but He is preparing a city (Hebrews 11:16; Revelation 21:2), and even a whole new creation (Revelation 21:1) for His children to inhabit forever. Truly "death has been swallowed up in victory," and Christians are free to focus upon all the eternal blessings purchased for us in Christ because He has removed all fear and danger from death (Psalm 16:8–11; John 10:28–30).

How could a loving God send anyone to hell?

I feel that I need to answer this question in two stages: first to address it in its implications (i.e., how it is worded), then to address it in its essence (what God does and why).

This question puts God in an unloving light before we've even begun. God is pictured as directly condemning people to hell who do not want to go there. The implications are that God is uncaring, harsh, and judgmental, while people are poor, innocent victims. This is quite far from the real situation and must be corrected by the proper Scriptures. First, God's efforts have not been focused on sending people to hell but on rescuing us from that fate (John 3:16; Romans 3:23–24). God does not delight in punishing the wicked but delights in mercy (Micah 7:18); He has moved heaven and earth to open an avenue for that mercy to the human heart (Romans 5:8). Second, the Bible reveals that humanity is not made up of poor innocents but hopelessly ruined sinners (Romans 3:10–11). As such the only thing we can earn from God is wrath and judgment (Romans 6:23). Even though hell is what we deserve, it is not what God wants to give us (John 3:16–18). God is not sending anybody to hell; He is mercifully holding back the end of time (2 Peter 3:9), waiting for us to respond to his offer of pardon and escape the penalty for sin.

Having responded to these misconceptions, I will list ways in which God's love is shown by faithfully carrying out the penalty for sins on those who refuse His abundant mercy and grace. The Bible teaches that it is loving to correct those who are in the wrong (Hebrews 12:6). The Bible also says that it is loving to uphold right and wrong clearly for the sake of those who are listening and learning (Romans 9:22–24). To sum up, those who end up in hell do so because they have rejected God's love, not because God is unloving.

I recently lost someone close to me. Where can I find words of comfort in the Bible?

It may not be easy for me to offer a satisfying answer to this question since grief can affect all of us in different ways. The best I can do is offer general guidelines and resources for grief, then list specific passages for various situations. I hope it helps.

One very beneficial source of comfort to us in times of grief is our relationships with others. Friends, family, a pastor, or a wise fellow believer can provide support and encouragement. The Bible shares with us the power of these relationships, commanding us to both give and receive that support and encouragement as needed (Galatians 6:2; 1 Peter 5:1–2). It doesn't have to be awkward and you can call them even if you haven't talked for a while. Let the conversation begin normally then share what's going on when it feels right. Even if you decide not to share your struggles it can still be nice to catch up with them.

Closely related to this is the resource of prayer. People will sometimes let us down, miss the hint, or not have time; God always listens. He is always there and you are free to "[cast] all your cares upon Him, for He cares for you," (1 Peter 5:7). The Psalms and other passages are full of people bringing all kinds of ugly or difficult emotions (even accusations!) to God in prayer. None of them get struck by lightning and all of them find what they need to keep moving forward, even if it's just for one more day.

Bible passages that specifically address the loss of loved ones (either through teaching or examples) include the account of the raising of Lazarus (helpful if we don't understand why someone had to die or have questions for God, John 11:1–44), the promise of the resurrection of the dead in 1 Thessalonians 4:13–18 and 1 Corinthians 15:35–58, and of course the passages that reveal God's nature as a shepherd are very comforting as well (Psalm 23; John 10:14–15, 27–30).

Can Christians be sent to hell?

Before I can directly answer this question, there are a few pink elephants that I need to address. By that I mean verses and passages that are cited as evidence for a certain view, but fail to hold up when examined in context. This should help alleviate some of the confusion commonly felt upon this issue.

Let me use Matthew 24:13 as an example. This verse is often quoted as evidence that Christians must 'endure to the end' in order to be saved. That is absolutely true. The catch is that "saved" in the context of Matthew 24 refers to being delivered from earthly perils (vv. 6–8), persecution (vv. 9–10), and deception (vv. 11–12). Eternal salvation from sin appears nowhere in the context!

Another commonly misunderstood text is Hebrews 6:4–8; a passage that lays out consequences for departing from the faith. The passage does seem to refer to genuine, born-again believers (vv. 4–5), and it clearly states the serious nature of falling away (v. 6). The question is; does it give eternal condemnation as the punishment for doing so? I do not believe that it does. Look at the illustration given in verses 7–8; A field of weeds is burned so that it may be replanted with beneficial plants. That would indicate that this passage is describing earthly consequences for sin (i.e., loss of rewards, loss of blessings, and even death; cf. 1 Corinthians 3:13–15; 1 Corinthians 11:29–30; Hebrews 12:5–8; etc.). Burning in the Bible is never enjoyable, but it is not always eternal (Cf. Zechariah 13:9 for another example).

Once we clarify these easily misunderstood passages the real answer of Scripture comes across loud and clear. Those who trust in Christ for salvation will not enter into eternal judgment (John 5:24), will never perish (John 10:28–29), and are safe from the Father's wrath (Romans 5:8–10). We have eternal life as a present possession (1 John 5:13), we are secure in the Father's love (Romans 8:31–39), and we have Christ as a present forgiver (1 John 1:9) and advocate (1 John 2:1). The earthly consequences for sin in the life of a Christian are clear and serious; but eternal condemnation in hell is not one of them.

Will the believers that die and go to heaven be able to have any relationship with nonbelievers?

I wish that I could provide a definite answer to this question. Unfortunately, the Bible leaves a lot of blanks concerning life after death, and the information we have is not particularly clear.

I know of only one passage that contains any mention of interactions between redeemed and condemned individuals after death, and it's very difficult to interpret. It is the account of the rich man and a poor beggar named Lazarus found in Luke 16:19–31, (This Lazarus is not the one Jesus raised from the dead). Lazarus the beggar suffers pain and hunger throughout his life while the rich man languishes in luxury. Upon their deaths their situations are reversed; the rich man is tormented while Lazarus is comforted "in Abraham's bosom." The rich man calls out to Abraham and is informed that the righteous dead are not permitted to pass over to the unrighteous (vv. 24–26), nor is there any need for individuals to return from the dead to warn the living (v. 27–31).

While this story does contain believers and unbelievers interacting after death over a "gulf" or "chasm" it is difficult to know what to make of it. Some see this account as a parable, which would make it a made-up story which shouldn't be taken literally in every detail. Others see it as an account of factual events; Jesus telling of two real individuals and sharing what happened to them when they died. There is no consensus among the experts, and I'm unaware of any further information in Scripture

This answer may leave you more confused than you were when you started, but sometimes pastors are just as confused as everybody else! If you are feeling lost or confused right now, I encourage you to go back to familiar passages like John 14:1–7, 1 Corinthians 15:50–57, 2 Corinthians 5:1–8, and 1 Thessalonians 4:13–18. These passages are both clear and reassuring; reminding us of the great peace and confidence we can have in Christ concerning life after death. Anything fuzzy or unclear regarding our eternal future can be entrusted to our Father and our Savior; no doubt all will be made clear in due time.

Does Hell have to be eternal? Couldn't it just be a temporary "time out"?

There are two reasons why an eternal punishment for sin is necessary. The first reason that hell is an eternal punishment is because sin does eternal damage. You see, we like to justify our sins and cast them in a harmless light. But the reality is that all sin is an eternal offense against God (Gen. 4:10; Matthew 5:21–48). It also causes deep and lasting harm to the sinner (Ezekiel 18:30–32), the victim of the sin (Exodus 22:23), society in general (Genesis 6:5), and God's creation (Romans 8:20–22). The only just and fair response to an eternal crime is an eternal punishment.

Sin is far more significant than goofing off in second grade and getting sent to the principal's office. All sin is, to some extent, addictive. Every step we take in the wrong direction steepens the slope and pitches us into even deeper sin; making it harder and harder to either stop or turn around (if you don't believe me, then try now to stop a sinful habit like speeding or gossiping). Without some remedy, this process is also eternal and will lead to more and more corruption and destruction (Romans 1:28–32). This means that every sin we commit does not just cause eternal damage; it also leads to greater sin, which leads to even greater eternal damage, and on to even greater sin.

Thankfully, God has provided us with a remedy for sin. Through Jesus Christ, God offers cleansing for corruption, pardon for all our wrongdoing, and redemption from the consequences. He is willing to bring His righteousness and power to bear; counteracting the destructive spiral and setting us on a path to righteousness and well-being. However, if a person refuses to be rescued from their sin there is no other alternative but to quarantine their corrupting influence by placing them in the only alternative to heaven: which is hell. The stakes are high: an eternal payment for eternal sin, without which we must suffer eternal punishment by enduring eternal torment. These truths are what make Christianity and the gospel so important!

What really happens when we die? Do we go straight to heaven? Do we go to purgatory? What does the Bible say?

It is hard to get a full and detailed understanding of the afterlife from Scripture. We are given a general picture and can have complete confidence in the basic elements (i.e., Believers will dwell with God forever, believers will be resurrected, etc.). But there are details about the sequence and circumstances that are debated within the church. For now, let me share some of the truths I believe to be taught clearly, and those that aren't we'll just have to wait to find out!

The first thing I think a believer can expect to happen when they die is to enter the presence of the Lord. In 2 Corinthians 5:1–8 the Apostle Paul compares our physical body to a house or tent that Christians should be ready and willing to give up, since we know we have a better one waiting for us: a "building from God". Paul declares that to be absent from the body (in other words; to die) means that we will be present with the Lord (v. 8). Jesus instructed His disciples to have the same confidence in John 14:1–6. Believers in Christ can rest assured that we will enter the Lord's presence from the moment we die.

Another truth we can be assured of is the resurrection from the dead (John 11:23–25; 1 Corinthians 15:20–23, 42–45, & 50–54). Believers are promised new physical bodies just like the Lord Jesus received (see John 20:26–29 & 1 John 3:2), which will be eternal and glorious, free from temptation, disease, and discomfort (Revelation 21:4). Early believers were so confident in the resurrection that they referred to death as merely "falling asleep," (Acts 7:59–60; 1 Thessalonians 4:13). Modern day believers can have the same confidence.

One more clear truth from Scripture is the Creation of a new heaven and earth (Revelation 21:1). Contrary to popular belief, the Bible doesn't teach that believers will live forever with God in Heaven. Instead, God and man will return to a newly created earth and dwell there eternally (Revelation 21:6–7). God is not going to abandon the earth to brokenness and futility forever; He's going to recreate it.

4

PRAYER

Can I pray without talking
or does it have to be out loud?

PRAYER CAN BE OUT loud or you can pray just thinking the words to yourself. We know that Hannah prayed without talking when she asked God for a son because it made the High Priest think she was drunk (1 Samuel 1:12–14)! Yet her prayers were answered. God knows the thoughts of our heart (Jeremiah 17:9–10; Mark 2:6–8) and every detail of our lives, both seen and unseen (Matthew 10:29–31). Jesus even advised his disciples to pray secretly so that no one could hear (Matthew 6:5–6), because even when no one else hears us, God still does! So we can have confidence that He hears our prayers even when no one else does.

I'd like to take this question one step farther though and talk about some guiding principles for how we should pray. We have many alternatives to choose from: we can pray silently or out loud. We can pray standing, sitting, kneeling, or walking. We can pray together and by ourselves (this article could be a Dr. Seuss book!). Even though there is no one perfect way to pray, we can learn ways to aid our prayers by matching our manner of prayer with the situation. For example, I've found that kneeling with closed eyes and a bowed head is helpful during times when I need to express humility to God (James 4:10). But when I'm driving out to an emergency situation, that wouldn't be the best time to close my eyes, fold my hands, and bow my head! Instead, that would be a great time to offer up a short, silent, prayer to God for His guidance and protection.

This is subjective and we are all free to experiment to find what works for us. Just remember that our location, posture, and manner of praying can affect our attitude and approach. Matching the right method with a given situation can help us pray effectively in all kinds of situations (1 Thessalonians 5:17).

I'm not a Christian, can I still pray?

When most people today speak about prayer they usually mean "to talk to God." But there is another meaning for prayer that is more common in the Bible, and it is the idea of bringing a petition or request to Him. Understanding this, I think the best answer to the above question is that unbelievers can both talk to God and bring petitions to Him, but only Christians can engage in these activities most fully and effectively.

There are many examples of people addressing God before committing themselves to Him in faith. Some of the more notable examples are Saul/Paul in Acts 9:10–11, as well as Cornelius in Acts 10:1–2. Also, since prayer is the easiest and most common means of expressing faith in Christ, any unbeliever can pray to *become* a Christians at any time (Romans 10:9)!

However, we are all born with problems in our nature which make prayer very difficult for those who haven't been born again. Before we are saved, the Bible describes us a spiritually dead or unresponsive toward God, stained with sin, and having various wrong perspectives of God that makes it nearly impossible to understand His ways or even perceive Him at all (Ephesians 2:1–3; 2 Corinthians 4:3–4)! The blood of Christ is the only thing that can correct these problems and enable us to interact with God freely and fully (Romans 5:1; etc.). The right to bring petitions to God is a privilege that the Bible reserves primarily for priests. In the Old Testament God established two different priesthoods (the order of Melchizedek and the Levitical priesthood) whose members had the responsibility of bringing the needs of the people before God. In the New Testament, that privilege and responsibility is extended to all Christians, who are called "priests of God," and a royal priesthood (1 Peter 2:9).

The Bible tells us clearly that God invites all of us to "draw near to Him in faith." God desires all of us to approach Him and interact with Him; He desires relationship with His beloved creation, and that includes both believers and unbelievers. Of course, the most important step that we can take towards God is to pray the prayer of faith and acceptance that causes our sins to be forgiven and us to be born again.

Can I pray even though I haven't gone to church for a long time?

Receiving God's mercy and help in time of need does not depend in any way upon your church attendance. Neither does it depend upon how much money you've given to charity, the quality of your life choices, nor your personal 'goodness.' That being said, the Bible does list some conditions that must be fulfilled before we can enter God's presence with confidence. I will list some of these below:

The most important thing you need before you seek God's face is humility. Pride and self-reliance are not only extremely offensive to God, they are also contrary to the spirit of prayer. We cannot genuinely ask God for help as long as we are pretending that we don't need help, or that we've got it all under control. Be real! Through prayer we enter the presence of the Almighty: humble yourself before Him (James 4:10).

The second thing you will need is forgiveness. You see, the Bible describes us all as sons of disobedience and children of wrath (Ephesians 2:2–3), born with a desire to live in self-reliance and reject God (Psalm 51:5–6). If we never change our manner of thinking by trusting in Christ, then, not only are we disqualified from effective prayer (Psalm 66:18), but we are barred from eternal life (Revelation 21:27).

One last helpful tip is to remember Who we are talking to. The Bible tells us who God is: our Maker (Psalm 100:3), the Sovereign Ruler of the Universe (Psalm 103:19), and our Judge (Psalm 50:6). But if we have trusted in the mercy God has shown us in Christ then He is also our adopted Father (Ephesians 1:5), Savior (1 Timothy 2:3), Refuge (Psalm 62:8), and help (Psalm 46:1). Even though we could never earn the help that we needed from God, Christ earned it for us upon the cross. Now believers can boldly approach the throne of grace for mercy and help (Hebrews 4:16), knowing he has promised us all we need for life and godliness (2 Peter 1:2–3), casting all our cares upon Him because He cares for us (1 Peter 5:6–7).

How should I pray about something like cancer as a Christian?

Let's start by asking what we want out of our prayer. Is there a specific outcome to your situation that you want (i.e., healing from cancer)? Are we seeking inner peace and wellbeing? Or do we simply want God to show up in our lives? There is no right or wrong answer here, the specific desire will simply determine the approach we take in our prayer. Take a moment to clearly determine your desire.

There is absolutely nothing wrong with wanting something specific and humbly bringing a request to God. Christians have the right to ask our Heavenly Father for things, even things not directly promised by Scripture (Hebrews 4:16; 1 Peter 5:7). If that's what you want to do, then simply bow your head and ask God for what you want. Think of it like a teenager asking to borrow his parent's car: you can ask, but your loving Father has the final say and He will do what is best for everyone in the situation.

If you are a Christian and you're lacking peace and rest, then it's important to seek that resolution and rest through prayer. Ask yourself what you are anxious about (Philippians 4:6), cast that care upon God (1 Peter 5:6–7), trusting Him to resolve that situation by His gracious power (Romans 15:13), and the peace of God will return (Philippians 4:7).

Whatever the details of your unique situation, we know from Scripture that God graciously works in the life of all those who are called by His name (Psalm 27:13; Romans 8:28). Bringing requests before God's throne of grace (Hebrews 4:16) is a powerful tool and a wonderful privilege. Ask in faith (James 1:6), ask on the authority of Christ's name (John 14:13–14; 1 John 5:14–15), commit yourself to the Lord (Psalm 27:4–5) and He will carry out His work!

5

BIBLE STUDY BASICS

**I think the Bible is huge and hard to read, but if I wanted to
read it where would I even start?**

THE BIBLE IS A big book, and it can be quite daunting to know
where to begin. The good news is that there are a couple of facts
about the Bible that can help us to find a good place to start. The
first fact is that the Bible isn't really one book; it is a collection of
(roughly) 66 different "books" or writings. It is perfectly proper to
read each book of the Bible individually, and these smaller books
are far easier to get through. In fact, over half of the books in the
New Testament are around the same size as a magazine article!

Another fun fact about the Bible is that it is made up of different genera; it isn't all one kind of literature! This means that we
can select our Bible reading based on the needs or preferences of
the day. No matter what we are feeling or going through, there
is a Bible passage that meets our needs! In the mood for quick,
straight-forward instructions for life? Read an Epistle like Ephesians or 1 Peter! Do you enjoy poetry? Read the Psalms! Want
something the size of a short novel? How about the true story of
David in 1 Chronicles, or Jesus in the Gospel of Mark or John? If
you prefer a shorter story, try the book of Ruth or Jonah! Once

you're ready to go deep you can wrestle with the big questions of life in the narrative of Job or start exploring the messages of the Old Testament Prophets!

My advice to anyone who is starting from square one in the Bible is to open it up to the table of contents, select a book based on the criteria in the above paragraph, and then read that book from its beginning on. Don't feel like you have to finish: if you're getting bogged down, try a different spot! Remember as you are reading that this is a living Book (Hebrews 4:12) and a message from God (2 Timothy 3:16–17). So be alert as you go through for anything that seems to jump off the page at you; God speaks through His Word!

Is reading a book about the Bible as good as reading the Bible?

It depends! A steak dinner is a wonderful and filling meal, but I don't expect my one-year-old daughter to manage it on her own. She is at an age where she still needs milk; food which has been processed and broken down into a form that she is able to digest. Teaching (whether books, sermons, or Bible studies) from good and qualified Christian teachers is a lot like mother's milk, and is even called milk in the Bible (1 Corinthians 3:1–3; Hebrews 5:12). Teachers seek to carefully break down the life-giving Truth of Scripture and present it in ways that are easier for us to comprehend.

One danger involved in this process is that it places distance between the source of Truth and the recipient. Just as water picks up sediment and contaminants as it flows away from the pure mountain spring, so also teaching can become less powerful and pure as it moves away from the Bible. Some "Christian teachers" are not as careful as they should be about keeping their teaching pure. So then, care must be taken to make sure that our teachers are giving us the Truth (2 Timothy 4:3–4).

This is one of many reasons why it is so important for Christians to be connected with a good, Bible-teaching Church with a godly pastor. A good pastor will provide the milk of clear teaching while also helping a Christian reach maturity so that they can test Christian teaching (including his own!) against the Word (Hebrews 5:14). In the meantime, the Church family and the Pastor can help an individual to test the teaching that is available and stay connected to life-giving Truth.

This does not mean that Christians should never read books that have errors or wrong thinking; we'd be back to only reading the Bible! We must remember that while the Bible is the only source of pure and unpolluted Truth, other books can be read so long as they are tested against that standard and taken with a grain of salt! Christian books by trustworthy authors can be extremely helpful, for both new and mature Christians. But it is vital for us to gain discernment and understanding of the Bible as soon as possible, so that we are not led astray by wrong teaching.

How do you tell if someone is teaching falsely?

The Bible offers two basic tests for truth: agreement with God's Word and the character of the teacher. As the Nation of Israel was entering the Promised Land God warned them about people who would seek to lead them astray. In order to prepare them to face this He commanded the Israelites to memorize and study His Word constantly, then compare it with what others are teaching. Any teaching that did not match up was false (Deuteronomy 11:16–21). This advice is repeated to God's people throughout the Bible (Psalm 1:1–2; Psalm 119:105; 2 Timothy 2:15; etc.).

Christ added an additional tip by telling His disciples, "You will know [false teachers] by their fruits." (Matthew 7:15–20) Those who live by the truths of God experience peace, rest, blessing, and strength of character; they are compared to a strong and healthy tree by the riverside (Psalm 1:3; Jerimiah 17:7–8). Just like you wouldn't take financial advice from a person up to their eyeballs in debt, so also you shouldn't listen to a teacher who is ungodly or unwise in their character. Genuine character can be hard to spot, however, so we must be patient and careful when searching for it.

Let me break these ideas down into some practical tips. First, learn to 'filter' the messages you are being given, never accept something as true until you've tested it yourself or run it by someone you trust. If someone uses Scripture to back up their perspective, look up the references. Are they twisting the verses or are they using them in context? Also, seek out people with godly character and spend time around them; absorb their knowledge and let that character rub off on you! Most importantly, stay connected with a good Bible-teaching church! Part of a pastor's job is to help his congregation avoid wrong and harmful ideas. If something doesn't seem right; ask your pastor or another mature believer!

Some Bible passages tell us to "pester" God with our prayers, others say that we should avoid vain repetition and just have faith; what gives? How often should we ask God for what we want?

First let me say that it's normal to see a tension between different Bible passages that address a given topic. If I tell one person to drive west to get to Mankato Kansas, then tell another to drive east to get to the same place, it can seem like a contradiction. Until I tell you that the first person lives in Belleville and the second lives in Smith Center! Just like learning that Mankato is west of Belleville, east of Smith Center, and north of Jewel gives us the precise location of the town, so also examining various Bible passages *in context* can help us understand the precise will of God on a certain topic. In this instance; prayer.

One passage that addresses the frequency of our prayers is Luke 11:5–13. In it, Jesus makes an interesting comparison between God and a tired friend who yields to his neighbor because of his persistent asking. Jesus is arguing from the smaller to the greater; if even a grumbling and tired man will yield to persistence, how much more will our loving Heavenly Father speedily answer the pleas of his children (verses 11–13)? This passage tells us that God *does* reward persistence, and goes on to the familiar promise: "ask and you shall receive." (Verses 9–10)

The warning against *vain* repetition is found right before the Lord's prayer in Matthew 6:7. In this passage Jesus is warning us not to try to earn God's favor by mouthing holy words over and over. Jesus reminds us that our heavenly Father knows what we need before we ask him, and gives an example of a simple prayer to pray in faith.

So you see, these two passages really do approach the same truth from different directions. Luke shows us that we should pray persistently and in faith, Matthew teaches that we should not pray in legalism or HOLLOW repetition. No contradiction!

I read in Romans 5:12 that death and sin are a consequence of Adam's disobedience in the Garden of Eden. If sin is Adam's fault, then why are we still punished for it?

Great question! In order to understand the answer, we'll start with the relationship between human nature and human choice.

Theologians commonly refer to Adam and Eve as innocent in nature (as opposed to God who has a righteous nature). They were a blank page, as such their nature would be determined by their choices. Adam's decision to sin warped and corrupted his human nature, which was afterwards passed along to all his descendants (thus Romans 5:12).

This means that we are all born with a natural tendency towards and lust for sin (Psalm 51:5). It does not mean that we are forced to sin, however. We have the ability to choose, and even to go against our natural urges (Romans 2:14–15). This ability is called our will or human choice.

Think of Adam's created innocence like a table that is perfectly level and straight. Were you to place a marble in the middle of that table, it would stay there without much difficulty. But if the table were warped, the marble wouldn't stay. On the contrary, it would require constant vigilance and effort to keep it from rolling off. Doing the right thing with a warped, sinful nature is like keeping 50 marbles on a warped table; technically possible, but in reality, it is an unattainable standard. In the same way, Righteous living has become too difficult for us and we all fail time, and time, and time again (Romans 7:15).

So then, each human being is a tangled combination of victim and perpetrator. We inherited a sin nature and suffer from the sins of others; that makes us victims. But we also make deliberate choices to sin; so we are guilty too! Only God could've come up with a way to sort out this mess: fairly punishing sin while showing mercy to sinners. He did this through Christ (Romans 3:23–26). Those who accept Christ's payment for sin are forgiven, cleansed, and given a new nature in Christ (1 Corinthians 15:22; 2 Corinthians 5:17, 21). Those who reject Christ have reject God's fair offer of pardon, thereby demonstrating their guilt and removing any justification for evading punishment (John 3:18).

What does the phrase "Vengeance is Mine," says the Lord" really mean?

"Vengeance is mine," Is an oft repeated promise from God to right the wrongs that surround us in this world (Deuteronomy 32:35; Psalm 94:1; Romans 12:19). Any time we see wrong done to ourselves or others we can often feel a strong desire for payback or revenge. If we act on this desire outside of God's will the Bible calls it taking vengeance. While the Bible does not say that wanting justice is wrong it DOES tell us that we are not to take justice into our own hands (Romans 12:17–21). Instead, we must trust God to handle it; vengeance belongs to Him.

When we choose not to avenge ourselves, we remember that God did not judge us according to our own sins and show our willingness to extend others the same mercy (Matthew 18:23–35). We also "give place to the wrath of God." (Romans 12:19), giving Him an open field to handle the situation with perfect skill and justice. God can do this in many ways but His punishment always fits the crime perfectly (for an example of God's poetic justice see Haman's arrogant hatred in Esther 3:1–6, with his humble pie in Esther 6:1–11). We can also rest assured that God will reward us for our patience and faith, regardless of what happens to the offender (1 Peter 2:20–23).

God's hope and desire is that all would come to him for forgiveness and pardon (1 Timothy 2:3). However, He also knows when consequences for sin are needed, and as a loving Father and a righteous Judge we can trust Him to do what is best. Only God is wise enough to find the perfect balance between vengeance and grace in a given situation. This is why we must always leave payback in His capable hands.

Is there any rhyme or reason to the names of books of the Bible? Who decided the names?

There are indeed sensible reasons for why each book of the Bible ended up with the name it did. We aren't sure who decided the name for each book, but we do know that no book title was part of the original work. Unfortunately, the Bible's rich and diverse history resulted in a diverse array of methods for naming the different books, and there isn't a great deal of consistency to be found.

Many books of the Bible were named after the author (Isaiah–Malachi except for Lamentations, James–Jude, etc.). Paul's letters in the New Testament are named after their recipients: Romans, 2 Thessalonians, and so on (he wrote thirteen books of the New Testament so turning to "12 Paul" wouldn't have worked very well!).

Most of the Old Testament Narratives are named for their first principal character (i.e., 1 Samuel, Job, Esther and so on) or characters (Judges, 1 and 2 Kings, etc.). They can also be named for a significant event within the story (Genesis is the story of the beginning, Exodus records the exit of the Israelites from Egypt). Some books are named by their theme or subject (Psalms is a book of praise songs, Proverbs is a book of proverbs; 1 and 2 Chronicles are chronicles of Israel's history. No rocket science here!).

Some titles of Bible books are actually longer than the names we typically use. For example, if you look at the Book of Romans your Bible will probably have some variation of this as a full title: "The Epistle of Paul to the Romans." The full title gives you the type of writing (epistle), the author (Paul), and the recipients (the Romans). The Books of Acts is typically given the full title, "The Acts of the Apostles," which gives a little more clarity as to the subject of the book

Christians who wish to learn more about the Bible could consider investing in a Study Bible. It contains helpful information about the title of each book, the author, date of writing, and more. You can also see if your church has a library with study resources in it, or talk to your Pastor to get more information.

Do the chapter and verse numbers in the Bible have any special significance? Who assigned the numbers? Why don't they seem to fit right in the Bible?

You are correct in saying that the chapter and verse divisions in our Bibles are different than how we commonly think of chapters today. To explain, let's start with some history!

The decision to put chapter divisions in the Protestant Bible was first made by a man named Stephen Langton around 1227 A.D. This was over 1,100 years after the Bible was completed. They were introduced with the intention of making it easier to refer to specific passages, even when different Bible versions were being used. A Jewish Rabbi named Nathan would introduce verses into the Hebrew Bible in A.D. 1448. And a man named Robert Estienne borrowed those verse divisions for the protestant Old Testament and subdivided the New Testament in a similar fashion.

This hugely simplified the finding of specific passages of Scripture. Imagine if a pastor had to ask you to thumb through the entire book of John for the words, "God so loved the world," rather than simply pointing you to John chapter 3 and verse 16! The chapters and verses serve their purpose of aiding in the navigation of Scripture.

While this system is quite helpful, it is not perfect. Some of the divisions are in very awkward places. Some unnecessarily divide the flow of a passage (i.e., Colossians 3:25—4:1), while others even break a thought mid-sentence (John 7:53—8:1)! The divisions are works of individuals, and often reflect their priorities or perspectives (Stephen Langston evidently knew some disobedient children because he put parental obedience right at the top of Ephesians chapter 6!).

Understanding the background and purpose of the Bible's chapters and verses can help us decide the best way to put them to use. It may not always be sensible to read the Bible by its chapter or verse divisions. Most modern Bibles contain headings and paragraph divisions, which seek to follow the biblical flow of thought more closely. If your Bible contains these then it can be more helpful to read from heading to heading, rather than reading chapter-by-chapter, or reading a certain number of verses a day.

Somebody told me that we cannot know that we are saved because Ecclesiastes 3:21 says that we cannot know whether spirits go up or down. Is that true?

It has often been said that a Bible text without context is nothing but a pretext. If a person cuts a verse of Scripture away from its context, they can twist it's meaning to support all kind of outlandish ideas! This is why those who genuinely desire to know the message of God's Word must learn to look at context! Let me use this verse (Ecclesiastes 3:21) as an example.

If we want to thoroughly understand a verse of the Bible the best way to start is to understand the book that it's a part of. And, typically, the best place to find the purpose of the book is at the beginning. We discover from the opening verses of Ecclesiastes that it was written as a discourse on the limits of human wisdom and the futility of life from a purely earthly perspective (Ecclesiastes 1:13–14). The author recorded his life-long search for meaning in various pursuits: wealth, worldly success, knowledge, pleasure, accomplishments, and more (Ecclesiastes 2:1–11). After trying everything he concludes that the only source of real meaning and happiness is enjoying good (Ecclesiastes 3:12–13), and fearing God (Ecclesiastes 12:13–14).

When we move into the immediate context (Ecclesiastes 3:18–22) we find the author lamenting man's limited perspective. We cannot see or perceive what happens after death. We have no direct perception of spirit, the only thing we can observe *using only human wisdom*, is that people die just like animals do.

The important thing to keep in mind with this passage is that the author considers all of this without any reference to God's Revelation! He is trying to figure life out on his own and that is impossible! This is why it was so necessary for God to send his Word to us; to reveal to us things that we otherwise would never have known. Humanity has no direct perception of the human spirit and no reliable way to see what happens after we die. But God has the birds-eye-view and has told us what will happen if we only believe (John 3:16; 2 Corinthians 5:1–8).

I went to a different Church and the preacher's Bible was different from mine. Why are some Bibles different from others? Which version is actually the Word of God?

The full theological answer to the question; "What is the word of God?" would be this: the Word of God is made up of the writings set down by holy men under the inspiration of the Holy Spirit (2 Peter 1:21), which were originally perfect and without error (2 Timothy 3:16–17).

Hopefully, this seems straightforward enough. However, there are a couple of challenges presented to those who would like to read God's word today. The first is that the original manuscripts were written in Hebrew, Aramaic, and Greek. The second is that we do not have the original texts; we have thousands of copies of the originals. While, in general, these copies are remarkably well preserved and agree with each other to an unheard-of degree, they still have varying degrees of consistency and accuracy. However, many biblical scholars working over many decades have used the various copies to determine the text of the original with around 99 percent certainty, which is unbelievably good work for a piece of historical literature over 2000 years old!

These twin challenges (translating 3 ancient languages into modern English, and sorting through thousands and thousands of copies to determine the precise wording of the originals) accounts for most of the variation between our modern English versions. I have a great deal of respect for the hard work that many faithful men and women are putting into giving us accurate and readable translations of the Word of God. We even have the benefit of reading a passage in multiple versions, which can help us get the full sense of the original message.

Before Jesus Christ was born, how were people saved?

A central teaching throughout Scripture is that eternal life is, and always has been, obtainable only by grace and through faith. Ever since Adam and Eve sinned in the garden of Eden, humanity has been unable to earn forgiveness or eternal life on our own (Romans 3:10–12). Only those who trust in God's mercy and forgiveness can hope to enter a right relationship with Him and gain eternal life (Romans 4:5).

Paul makes this point in Romans chapter four, where he gives two examples of individuals in the Old Testament who were saved by trusting in God. The first is Abraham, who "believed God, and it was accounted to him for righteousness" (Romans 4:3, cf. Genesis 15:6). The second is David who wrote several psalms about the joy of undeserved forgiveness (Romans 4:6–8, cf. Psalm 32:1–2). To these we can add Noah, who "found grace in the eyes of the Lord," (Genesis 6:8), and also the Prophet Habakkuk who declared that "the just [one] shall live by his faith," (Habakkuk 2:4). A fun fact about this last verse is that it was the verse that opened Martin Luther's eyes to justification by faith and sparked the Protestant Reformation; and it's in the Old Testament!

Because the same God reigns in both New and Old Testaments His program of salvation has always been the same. Christ's death covered all sins, past, present, and future. Hallelujah!

Do you believe there is such a place as Hell?

Perhaps a better question would be, "Does the Bible clearly teach the reality of hell?" or "Does Jesus Christ believe in hell?" The perspective of God's inspired word and the God-man Himself are much more authoritative than any pastor's opinion. However, the answer to all three of these questions is the same: "yes!"

Both the Bible in general and Jesus Christ in particular repeatedly teach about a place of everlasting punishment and torment. It is referred to as hell, the outer darkness, and the lake of fire. For sake of space, I will give just three important teachings about hell from Scripture: first, it was created to be a place of punishment for the Devil (which is why it is so terrible; see Matthew 25:41). Second, we are told that it is a horrible place that no one in their right mind would ever want to go to (Matthew 22:13; Revelation 20:10). Finally, we are also told that God does not want anyone to perish or go to hell (1 Timothy 2:3–6; 2 Peter 3:9), in fact He was so committed to rescuing us from hell that he sent His only begotten Son as a sacrifice to take our place so that we could spend eternity with God in Heaven (John 3:16).

Who chose and compiled the books of the Bible?

The simplest way to explain how we got the Bible is to say that the 66 books that make up the Protestant Bible were inspired by God and then recognized by believers; first by Jewish believers in Old Testament times and finally by the early Church. Books of the Old Testament were verified by the miraculous works God did through the writers, by supernatural predictions which came to pass, and by conformity to books previously accepted (i.e., the psalms match the teachings found in Genesis-Deuteronomy).

The task of confirming the inspired books of the New Testament fell to church leaders during the 2nd century A.D. To do this the early church had to comb through many contemporary Christian writings; sifting them for evidence of inspiration. They wanted to be sure that the works they were testing had been written by an apostle or someone close to an apostle, that it matched with the teachings of the apostles, and that it bore evidence of the Spirit's life-changing work. The early church was able to use these criteria to detect several false writings (such as the so-called "Gospel of Thomas") and eventually finalize the list of books that would be considered "the Canon of Scripture."

God could have forgiven all sins Himself, so why did he send his son to a torturous death to forgive sins?

I can think of at least 3 things that were accomplished by the Cross that could not have been accomplished any other way. First, sin was publicly and fully punished. We have in the gospels a record of the severity of sin and the kind of punishment it warrants. Even though we do not have to suffer that penalty, the fact that the punishment was meted out to Christ in real history is a sobering message to all about the severity of sin. Without the cross it would be all too easy to take sin as "not that big of deal."

Second, the cross was an outlet for the wrath of God (Ephesians 5:5–6). God is patient and forbearing, and while he has withheld judgment on the earth for millennia, all sin offends Him and wrecks the perfect creation that was made as an expression of His skill and worthiness (Romans 1:18). Patience is one of the few attributes of God that is NOT infinite, so the bill had to come due sooner or later. By agreeing to bear the brunt of God's wrath on our behalf Christ opened the door for us to escape (Romans 5:1; 1 Thessalonians 1:10).

But there is also an upside to the Cross; it demonstrated God's unconditional love and grace to a greater extent than anything else could. The suffering and hardship of the Cross reveals just how much God loves us (John 3:16), in that He was willing to extend grace and a way of escape; even to His enemies! The value of our salvation is shown by the high price God was willing to pay for it (1 John 3:16). This has many implications for the believer today (1 Peter 1:17–19).

The central conflict in the story of Scripture has been how a perfect, holy, and just God could be both "Just and the justifier of the one who has faith in Christ Jesus," (Romans 3:26). The Cross was the perfect solution to this thorny problem; and that is precisely why God chose it.

Is the death penalty for crimes justified in the Bible? Under what circumstances?

There is a great deal of guidance in the Bible regarding capital punishment, and it begins in the time of Noah. In Genesis 6–8 we read that universal violence and moral rot made it necessary for God to wipe the slate clean by a global flood and start over (Genesis 6:5–7). In Genesis 9 God tells Noah what must be done to prevent the world from becoming that corrupt again: humanity must learn to police itself through government. Central to this responsibility was the institution of capital punishment (Genesis 9:5–6).

Life is a gift from God and humanity is made in God's Image. This is why stealing life from a human being is such a serious matter (Exodus 20:13). The punishment required by God for murder is the death of the guilty man (Genesis 9:6; Exodus 21:12). This provides justice to the victim's family (Genesis 4:10; Exodus 21:23; Numbers 35:33), a deterrent against future offences, and "puts away the evil act from the land," (e.g., Deuteronomy 21:21).

Exceptions to this 'life for life' rule are found in the Old Testament Law. The stipulations for those exceptions were carefully laid out (e.g., Exodus 21:12; Exodus 22:2; Numbers 35:9–11; etc.). In addition, capital punishment was required in the Nation of Israel for kidnapping (Deuteronomy 24:7), rape (Deuteronomy 22:25), and adultery (Deuteronomy 22:22), to name just a few.

Applying these verses to modern government must be done carefully. It isn't as simple as cutting and pasting Deuteronomy into our code of laws, nor should we completely ignore the Old Testament as barbaric or obsolete (Romans 3:31; 1 Timothy 1:8). Instead, those seeking to establish justice in their lives must sift the Bible for timeless principles of justice, then discern how those principles can be lived out in their unique setting and circumstances (e.g., 1 Corinthians 9:8–12 with Deuteronomy 25:4).

This student of the Word considers capital punishment to be a practicable principle of justice that governments can draw on today. It is the very basis for human government in both Old and New Testaments (Genesis 9:5–6; Romans 13:1, 4). Also, we are told that inadequately punishing sin causes immorality to flourish and a blood debt to accumulate in the land. Eventually it becomes necessary for God to step in and execute justice Himself; and that is never pleasant.

The Bible says, "Blessed are the meek." When I look around at real life it doesn't seem like the meek are being blessed, it seems like they're getting passed over. How can this verse be true when experience seems to show the opposite?

The truths of God's Word often contradict what we think we know about how the world works. This forces us to choose between trusting ourselves or trusting God. Christ's teaching about meekness in Matthew 5:4 is a great example.

To begin, let me first explain what it means to be meek. In the Bible meekness means to be humble and understated; to exercise self-control even if it means getting less than you deserve. This flies in the face of our modern perspective, which preaches self-promotion and selfishness as the real way to get ahead and be blessed. We have turned pride and self-promotion into an art form; writing resumes and Facebook posts proclaiming all our gifts, achievements, and abilities. Yet the Word of God remains; "Blessed are the meek, for they will inherit the earth."

Now, the Bible does not ignore reality. Many passages of Scripture acknowledge that you can enjoy temporary (even lifelong) benefits through being selfish and pushy. All sin has temporary benefits, and many are deceived by those benefits into ignoring morality and doing whatever it takes to get ahead (Psalm 73:3–9). Yet the Word of God still says; "Blessed are the meek, for they will inherit the earth."

Ultimately, the only way to understand the blessing of meekness is in the context of judgment. Bad people do bad things and it seems to work out for them for a time. But one day God is going to judge all those who broke the rules in "un-meekness." All the corner-cutters, all the cheaters, the liars, the thieves, and the proud will be removed from the earth (Psalm 73:12, 18–20; Revelation 21:7–8). They will pay in blood for every blessing that they stole from the deserving. In that day the meek will inherit the earth, because the meek will be the only ones left.

Is there any need to study the Old Testament since the teachings of Jesus are in the New Testament?

Great question! The Bible is divided into Old Testament and New Testament (see the table of contents in your Bible). But many people struggle with reading the Old Testament since many passages do not seem to relate to our lives as easily as those of the New Testament. However, we must be careful not to think that the Old Testament lacks the teachings of Jesus. In fact, when teaching his disciples after being raised from the dead, Jesus revealed to them "in ALL the Scriptures the things concerning Himself." (Luke 24:27).

There are all kinds of ways that the gospel of Jesus is foreshadowed in the Old Testament; from detailed predictions about Jesus' life made hundreds of years in advance (Isaiah 53:1–9; Micah 5:2), to subtle foreshadowings that only made sense once Christ had come (compare John 3:14–15 with Numbers 21:4–9). Tracking down all these "Easter eggs" is one of my favorite ways to study the Bible!"

Many wonderful and life-changing truths are hidden in Old Testament passages (Like Psalm 23, and Isaiah 40:21–31). And even though it takes a little more leg work to unearth them, the reward is more than worth the effort!

6

BIBLE TRIVIA

Genesis 3:14 says that God cursed the serpent to crawl on the ground. Does this mean that snakes had legs before they were cursed?

THE LANGUAGE OF GENESIS 3:14–15 is not precise; it could be saying that the serpent didn't crawl prior to the curse, but the text does not necessarily demand that interpretation. Teachers have taken both positions throughout history, and I don't think any significant truth is affected by either perspective. Personally, I tend to lean slightly towards the perspective that snakes have always slithered and were not originally created with legs. I have two reasons for thinking so. First, I see crawling on the belly as a restoration of created order. Creeping things like serpents are placed at the bottom of two separate lists of land animals in Genesis 1, I believe that God was simply returning the serpent to his place in creation after the serpent asserted authority over Adam and Eve.

My second reason for doubting that the serpent had legs is biological. Snakes are designed to slither; their spines are flexible and made to move along the ground. A number of changes would be required for the serpent to change from a quadruped to a "no-ped." God could certainly have made all the necessary changes to make the serpent leg-less, it just seems to be an overcomplicated explanation when a simpler perspective is so available.

However, I don't consider either argument to be conclusive and have no problem at all with those who have a different perspective.

I noticed that some of the Psalms contain the word Selah. Do you know what that means?

The precise meaning of the Hebrew word "Selah" is one of the great unsolved mysteries of the book of Psalms. It is difficult to translate because it appears without direct context or definition, leaving scholars very little information to go on.

To probe deeper we need some background facts about the Book of Psalms. Psalms was essentially the worship book for the nation of Israel. Because of this, it comes with various musical notations and references in the text (Psalm 4 has the following notation; "To the chief musician, with stringed instruments). Some of these notations indicated a preferred tune or instrument to use when singing the psalm (Psalm 69 was set to the tune, "to the lilies"). Others indicate the style of the Psalm (praise, lament, prayer, and so on).

The word Selah, however, often appears within the Psalm itself (see Psalm 4:2 and Psalm 4:4). This could indicate a musical interlude or pause, or perhaps it simply indicates the close of a verse. Even Bible scholars don't have much more to go on than guesses.

The best guess I've heard is that the word Selah was written any time the Psalmist wanted the listener to stop and absorb what was just sung. Selah was probably a chance to meditate; to let the message of the song sink in rather than just going in one ear and out the other. Readers of the Psalms today can respond similarly by pausing their reading when they encounter the word and reflecting on the meaning of the psalm. Many readers (myself included) find that this makes the reading of the Psalms much more meaningful and enriching.

What are the gospels and how are they different from epistles?

Great question! Because the Bible is such a unique book there are many facts about it that we can only know by asking. We should never be afraid to ask something we don't know. Asking is, after all, the only way for us to find out!

The first four books of the New Testament (Matthew, Mark, Luke, and John) are commonly referred to as the four gospels. Mark even refers to his work as a gospel in the first verse. The fact that they are called "gospels" means is that these accounts are announcements of good news. We could call them testimonials or witness statements to the character and work of Jesus Christ. They present 4 distinct narrative accounts of Christ's earthly ministry and teachings, and all four include detailed accounts of His arrest, trial, crucifixion, and resurrection.

We know from the gospels that Christ, after His resurrection, sent out His closest followers to preach the good news and form the church (Matthew 28:18–20). These eleven men (joined later by the Apostle Paul and others) would spend the rest of their lives doing just that. At various points along the way, they would write letters to different groups of Christians. Some of those letters, or epistles, were preserved as special examples of the apostle's teachings. Later those epistles would be collected, along with the gospels, to form what we call the New Testament.

Someone told me that the Psalms are poetry, but they don't rhyme or seem to make much sense. Do they rhyme in a different language?

This confused me as well for a great many years! For a long time, I assumed that, since the Psalms were written in Hebrew, that they must rhyme when read in the original language. But the truth is even better and far more exciting than that!

Hebrew poetry does not function by connecting similar sounds line by line, instead Hebrew poets would use the lines of their poetry to compare concepts. Hebrew poetry rhymes ideas!

Let me give you one of my favorite examples. Psalm 1:1 says "How blessed is the man; who does not walk in the counsel of the wicked; nor stands in the path of sinners; nor sits in the seat of scoffers" (The line breaks are indicated by a semi-colon). Each line after the first warns of a particular activity we must avoid if we wish to be blessed in life. The poetic connection of ideas is found between the similar kinds of people we should avoid (wicked/sinners/scoffers), and in the imagery of a person distracted from a journey; progressively walking, standing, then sitting as we move through the verse. A strong contrast is then introduced in verse two: rather than being swayed and distracted by ungodly company, the blessed man "delights in the Law of the Lord (the Bible); and in His law he meditates day and night."

The repetition, imagery, and comparison used by Hebrew poets in Psalms and Proverbs allowed them to be extremely clear and precise in communication. And, best of all, Hebrew poetry can be appreciated in any language! Why don't you go on in Psalm 1 and see if you can spot the five descriptions of the blessed man in verse three? The poetry of Hebrews is striking, memorable and accessible for anyone to read!

What do we know about the Christmas Star?

The term "star" in the Bible can refer to any small heavenly body. Shooting stars, planets, and galaxies would have all been referred to as stars in biblical times, because they all look the same to the naked eye. The sun and moon would not have been thought of as stars, even though we now know that the sun is a kind of star, it wasn't classified as such back then. So then, when the magi claimed to have seen the star of the newborn king of the Jews, shooting stars, galaxies, planets, and genuine stars are all possibilities to consider.

There is also a possibility that the star was some kind of miraculous or angelic event, separate from any natural explanation.

We can take these possibilities to Matthew 2:1–12 to see if the description in the passage rules any of them out. Verse 2 gives us very little definite information, only that they saw the star in the east (could mean the star was in the eastern part of the sky, that they were in the east when they saw it, or that they saw the star "in its rising"). We can also see that the magi interpreted this star to mean that the promised king of the Jews had been born.

Matthew 2:9–10 gives us more to go on. When the Magi are departing Jerusalem for Bethlehem, the star appears again: travelling south towards Bethlehem, and then stopping over the place where the child was. It is difficult to imagine any natural phenomenon like a comet doing all the things that the passage describes. While some think that a natural explanation is likely, personally I tend to lean more towards the star being some sort of supernatural event, like a miracle or angel.

In the end, however, the only thing we really need to know about the star is that it fulfilled its supernatural purpose in guiding the wise men to the Infant King they were seeking.

What are magi? Where did they come from?

The Greek word *Magoi* (Where we get our word "Magi") refers primarily to an ancient class of advisors who were known for their expertise and advice. While we meet some very dubious magi in the book of Acts (Acts 8:9–24; 13:6–12), the better sort of magi were (somewhat) reputable advisors in ancient Babylon, Persia, and later empires. They were considered experts in a variety of fields, but were particularly well known for astrology: the practice of foretelling events by the movement of the stars. While the Bible takes a very dim view of astrology (Isaiah 47:12–14) and most modern societies put little stock in it, it was considered an accepted practice in many ancient cultures, particularly in the Middle East. And it was also considered common for the birth of important persons to be heralded by different astronomical events.

This explains why no one in the story really bats an eye when the Magi show up in Jerusalem claiming that a star led them to seek a newborn Jewish King. They are taken seriously because they were experts in a practice considered genuine by many gentiles of the day. It is likely that these magi heard the Old Testament prophesies about a coming Jewish King (or Messiah) from believing Jews. When these magi beheld the star that announced the birth of the Messiah, they must have decided to witness this momentous event personally, and traveled west to Jerusalem.

The Magi are only one of many examples of God meeting seekers where they are and leading them towards the truth. While God did not approve of their practice, He did approve their heart, and sent them the answer to their search through a mechanism they would have understood (Jeremiah 29:13). God has many ways of leading people to the Truth, and He is working today, just as in the past, to lead people to a personal encounter with His Messiah; Jesus Christ.

When were the angels made?

The first angelic event that we have clearly timestamped is Satan's appearance in the Garden of Eden to tempt Eve (Satan was likely a fallen angel; Genesis 3:1; cf. Revelation 12:9). This means that several events on the angelic timeline must have already taken place by that point. Those events are: the creation of angels, Satan's prideful corruption into a fallen angel (Isaiah 14:12–14), his rebellion in heaven, His defeat, and his banishment to the earth drawing a third of the angels after him (Revelation 12:3–4, 7–9).

It is possible that angels were created during the 6 days of creation. Some argue this perspective by saying that God made everything in six days so he must have made angels within that time (Exodus 20:11). However, this is not very compelling since the Bible says that "God created the Heavens and the earth and all that is in them." As spiritual beings (Psalm 104:4), I wouldn't necessarily place angels within any of those categories.

A more likely possibility is that angels were created some time prior to the 6-day creation. We are told that angels were created to dwell with God in Heaven (2 Kings 22:19), and to worship Him (Hebrews 1:6; Revelation 5:11–13), also Job 38:4, 7 seem to indicate that "sons of God" were witnessing and rejoicing at God's creation acts (sons of God is another way to refer to angels; see Job 1:6).

Taking the whole counsel of Scripture as best I can, my best guess with the information available to me in Scripture is that angels were created sometime prior to the 6-day creation. However, we are told more clearly that angels minister to those who inherit salvation (Hebrews 1:14) and they are servants of God who do his will (Psalm 103:20)

Where was Jesus during the time between His death and resurrection?

If this is a question about Jesus' body between his death and resurrection, then it will be easy to answer. However, the question of what happened to Christ's Spirit after He died is an extremely complex question that remains unresolved even to this day. We will briefly discuss both issues here.

Physically, Christ's body was removed from the cross late Friday evening by Joseph of Arimathea (Luke 23:50–52). He placed Jesus' body in his own family tomb (Mark 15:46) because it was nearby and they had to work fast to be finished before the official beginning of the Sabbath at sundown (John 19:42). The tomb was placed under guard on Saturday (Matthew 27:62–66), and the guards remained until Sunday morning, when Jesus was raised from the dead and revealed to His disciples. It is wonderful how careful and detailed the gospel writers were; their four accounts are consistent, mutually supportive, and noncontradictory.

Information regarding Christ's spirit during the same period is much less clear and detailed. The only passage I know of that might possibly bear on this question is 1 Peter 3:18–20. This passage tells us that Christ "went and preached to the spirits in prison who formerly were disobedient in the days of Noah." What Christ preached, why He preached to these spirits specifically, and whether the spirits were human or angelic are all questions that have no biblical answer, as far as I know. Different biblical scholars have different perspectives, but since there is so little information to go on, we probably won't have a certain answer this side of heaven.

When I come across questions that are not answered by Scripture, I find it helpful to remember verses such as 2 Timothy 3:16 and 2 Peter 1:3. These verses remind us that all truths necessary for our life, well-being, and blessedness are provided to us by God and in Scripture. Truths that are not clearly taught in the Bible must not be necessary for us to know. We must wait patiently to find out the rest when we get to Heaven (1 Corinthians 13:12)!

How do dinosaurs fit into the Bible?
Were there dinosaurs on the ark?

When it comes to the question of dinosaurs in the Bible we have little information, but most of that information is drawn from one of the most reliable and trustworthy ancient documents in history: the book of Genesis.

When we look into Genesis, we find a narrative clear and detailed; containing genealogies, geographical locations, and the history of Israel's ancestors. It is clearly intended to be read as a historical account of real people, and is consistently treated as such by the Apostle Paul (Romans 5:14–15; etc.), the Apostle Peter (2 Peter 3:3–7), and the Lord Jesus Himself (Matthew 19:3–6). The account that it provides has been corroborated by countless archaeological digs and verified by Hebrew scholars.

This historical narrative offers a clear account of the origin of the created world and all the creatures that inhabit it. Genesis 1:24–25 tells us that 'all creatures that walk upon the earth' were made by God on the 6th day of creation, right before the creation of the first human couple (Genesis 1:24–26). As creatures that walked on the earth, dinosaurs would be included in this category, thus predating man by a matter of hours, not millions of years.

As some of the many created kinds of animals it is reasonable to also add dinosaurs to the list of animals destroyed by God in the Flood (which would explain why we have so many fossils of them! Genesis 6:17), as well as the pairs of "every created kind" included upon the ark (Genesis 6:19). What happened to the various created kinds after the Flood is not something which the Bible comments on in any detail.

Obviously, this contradicts several current scientific perspectives, which should not overly concern those convinced of the authority of Scripture. Scientific perspectives are constantly shifting and changing, what they are confidently proclaiming today will be replaced tomorrow. While Christians should not be dogmatic regarding our own imperfect perspectives, neither should we be swayed by the confident preaching of the scientific community; they have been wrong in the past, they will be shown to be wrong in the future. The only work that has an unimpeachable track record is Scripture itself; it is the unchanging rock upon which we can build our lives and perspectives.

What is a spirit? Is it different from your soul?

I might compare the terms "soul" and "spirit" to the terms "morals" and "ethics." The two words can overlap in meaning and be basically synonymous (compare John 12:27, with John 13:21 for example). However, at other times they are distinct in usage and differences can be drawn between them (1 Thessalonians 5:23; Hebrews 4:12).

Fundamentally, the word "spirit" in Scripture is drawn from Hebrew and Greek words with the sense of wind or breath; something that is there but cannot be easily understood or detected (John 3:8). So then "spirit" refers to something unseen but essentially real. This can be an attitude (Proverbs 16:18), a gift or ability (Exodus 28:3), an unseen being or angel (Psalm 104:4), the immaterial part of a human being (Psalm 146:4), or God Himself (Psalm 139:7).

The word "soul" is also drawn from the concept of breath, but it leans more toward the sense of a person's existence or life. Soul can mean our inner or immaterial being (Luke 12:19), which departs when we die (Matthew 10:28). It can also be used to describe an entire person (Ezekiel 18:20; Acts 2:41), or as a synonym for physical life (Luke 12:20). The Greek term can also mean our mind or rational self (Philippians 1:27).

The slight differences in meaning lead to slightly distinct usages for each term in Scripture. For example, God and the angels are almost universally described as spiritual, while the term "soul" is used more frequently for human beings. A concordance can be used to look up all of the places where each word is used if you would like to dig deeper into the distinctions between them. This was a great question!

I don't hear much about Jesus' siblings, did they grow up together? How did they feel about Jesus?

It's true that Jesus' siblings are somewhat difficult to spot in Scripture (see Matthew 13:55 for a list of their names). This is because the gospel accounts are not biographies in the modern sense but witness statements of the miracles and message of the Messiah. As such they focus on Jesus' ministry and not as much upon his family or upbringing.

However, we can use what we are given to piece together a few facts about Jesus family. Of course, Jesus was Mary's firstborn (Matthew 1:24–25; Luke 2:22–23), so the others must have been born after. Any guesses as to their family dynamics are solely speculation as none of the accounts of Jesus' early years mention his siblings. We are told that Jesus' brothers (technically half-brothers) did not believe in Him right away, probably persisting in their unbelief until after He was raised from the dead (John 7:1–5; 1 Corinthians 15:7).

Two of Jesus' brothers (James and Jude) do appear in the history of the early church. Apparently after encountering Jesus risen from the dead, James became a believer (1 Corinthians 15:7), and eventually an elder and influential leader in Jerusalem (Acts 15:3; Galatians 2:9), even writing a letter to scattered believers that we know as the Epistle of James. However, in his letter he does not call himself the Lord's brother, choosing the humbler title of bondservant to Christ.

While not mentioned in Acts, the writer of the epistle known as Jude is traditionally understood to be another brother of Christ. He also refers to himself solely as a bondservant of Christ and brother of James.

Jesus' half-brothers did not receive any kind of special privileges or recognition because of their relationship to Christ, either by God or by the early Church. However, it seems that at least a couple of them accepted the offer that was made to all mankind, that is to accept that their half-brother was really the Son of God, and to receive forgiveness of sins by believing in Him.

Why does the Catholic Bible have more books than the NIV Bible? Why aren't they the same? Which set of books is actually the complete Word of God?

The process of identifying which writings make up God's word was far more organic than many people realize. On several occasions over the first and second centuries the Church published lists of books that they considered authentic. While the church consistently condemned several non-authentic documents there was some variation on exactly which books were approved. Many books (Romans and Ephesians are two examples) appear consistently in every list. Some, like 2 Peter and Esther, appeared on some lists but not others. The 7 books which are included in the Catholic Bible but not Protestant were considered "helpful but not authoritative," by many early church leaders. The question on these extra seven books was essentially; "Where do we draw the line on Inspiration?"

The Church went back and forth about the seven apocrypha or deuterocanonical books for centuries. Some Bibles listed them in the appendix; others omitted them. The final decision to list them in the Canon of Catholic Bibles was made during the Council of Trent (A.D. 1545). This was after the Protestant Churches had separated from the Catholic Church.

Many Protestants (myself included) still consider the Deuterocanon to be interesting and helpful, both from a historical and Spiritual perspective. Just like modern writings from godly men and women which can be very beneficial to a person's walk with God. However, it is necessary for believers to have a standard of Inspired Truth (a canon) that we can hold these other works to, so that we can effectively discern right from wrong; Truth from error. Catholics include the 7 deuterocanonical books in their Canon; Protestants put them just on the far side of inspiration.

Are there prophets in the world today?

Fundamentally, to "prophesy" in the Bible means to "speak under the influence of someone or something else." It can refer to insane babbling (1 Samuel 18:10), speech inspired by evil spirits (2 Chronicles 18:18–22), faithfully communicating messages from God (Ezra 5:1), or recording God's messages, which would eventually become the books of the Bible (Hebrews 1:1).

Do any or all of these activities continue in modern times? Leaving insane babbling to one side, the New Testament warns believers to be on guard against false teachers and false prophets (Matthew 7:15; 1 John 4:1), these activities, unfortunately, are still very much present. When it comes to those claiming to have new revelation or messages from God the traditional perspective of the Church is that the Canon of Scripture was closed upon the death of the Apostles. Apostles and prophets formed the foundation of the Church (Ephesians 2:20), and once the foundation was completed their positions were no longer needed (1 Corinthians 13:8). Christians today are blessed with a personal relationship with God (1 John 2:20), the ministry of the Holy Spirit (John 14:25–26), and the completed Word of God (Psalm 119:105). Because we can receive God's message ourselves, God no longer needs a 'go-between' to deliver His word.

In short, if someone comes to you claiming to have a message or additional revelations from God they should be treated with extreme skepticism and caution (1 Thessalonians 5:21; 2 Cor. 11:13–15). Let your pastor know what is going on, and bring the Light of God's Word to bear on the message, exposing any errors that it holds.

Did God show Himself to His followers like Jesus did?

This question gives me an opportunity to share about one of my favorite Old Testament mysteries: theophanies. Taken by itself, it is hard to figure out whether people saw God in the Old Testament or not. Certain passages say that no one can see God and live (Exodus 33:18–20), while others record people seeing God; or at least a vision of Him (Exodus 24:9–11; Judges 6:22–23). Some passages speak of God as an invisible, omnipotent Being (1 Kings 8:27); others speak of Him appearing in human form (Genesis 18:1–2). How can we reconcile these ideas?

The solution to this mystery can be found in the New Testament, in the Gospel of John. John 1:12 explains that God the Father has never been seen, but it has always been the function of God the Son to reveal the Father to us in ways we can comprehend (John 14:8–9). So then, the occasions in the Old Testament where God was seen directly by His people must have been an appearance of Jesus Christ prior to His birth and earthly ministry. This is what theologians call theophanies. God shows himself to His followers in the same way in both the Old and New Testaments; through Jesus Christ!

Were there biblical laws before the 10 commandments?

I guess it depends on what you mean by biblical laws. God designed the universe to function according to certain fundamental laws; whether they be physical laws like gravity, motion, and thermodynamics, or moral laws like family, faith, and character. Living with a proper respect for these laws (i.e., not jumping off a cliff or changing God's design for family) has always resulted in blessings and fulfillment in life. The Bible refers to this respect for God's laws and right living as "righteousness" (a.k.a. right character). The Ten Commandments added a new layer to these fundamental laws by making righteousness a civic responsibility for the nation of Israel as well as fundamental for well-being in life (Deuteronomy 30:15). God did this for Israel to make the destructive effects of unrighteousness more clear, and also as a way to protect Israel from its harmful effects. More information on God's purpose for Israel's civic laws (including the Ten Commandments) can be found in Romans 3:19–24; Romans 7:7–12; and Galatians 3:21–25

Starting with Adam and Eve, did people marry their siblings in the Old Testament? If so, why?

This is a question that I have often been asked. First let me say that the historical account of Genesis does not explain where Cain got his wife, or why individuals like Abraham married close relatives (Abraham married his half-sister Sarah), or whether it was permissible for them to do so. In short, the Bible does not directly answer this question.

Because the authoritative word of God is silent on the subject, we are free to come up with a best-guess by drawing from scientific research and sanctified common sense. Genesis 5:4 tells us that Adam had other sons and daughters besides Cain, Abel, and Seth; it would be reasonable to assume that Cain and Seth took wives from this group, which would be their sisters. Some scientists who believe the Bible have suggested that the near-perfect condition of the human genome at that point in history may have prevented the harmful health conditions that result from more modern marriages between near relatives. This may be why we only see marriages between near relatives in the book of Genesis (as far as I know), and why incest was later forbidden by the Law of Moses around 1500 B.C. (Leviticus 18:6). There may be a better answer than this out there, however, we may have to wait until we get to heaven before we can know for sure!

7

APOLOGETICS

Is there any rational evidence for Christianity?

OH BOY, WHERE DO I start? The short answer is *yes*!!! Christianity is the most well attested belief system in the world. While many are unaware of it, I think there is more evidence in support of Christianity than any other belief system. That's why I'm a Christian! I personally own books 2" thick which are filled with evidence for the Christian faith. Obviously, I can't share all of it with you in a newspaper article so I will cut to the heart of the matter and try and present the rational core of Christianity with the space I have available

Christianity is unique among the belief systems of the world because it rests wholly and completely upon one verifiable historical event. The event is the resurrection of Jesus from the dead; disprove that and you disprove Christianity (1 Corinthians 15:15:14–18). I'm not worried, however, because Jesus' resurrection is by far the most validated and corroborated event in history.

I've mentioned in several past articles that we have 4 independent eyewitness accounts of the resurrection: the four gospels (which is far more than most ancient events whose authenticity we take for granted). In addition, we have a creed quoted by the

Apostle Paul in A.D. 56 (found in 1 Corinthians 15:1–8). This creed attests that Christ died, was buried, and arose from the dead, and attaches a list of people who had physically encountered the risen Christ. The list includes the twelve disciples, James the brother of Jesus (who was likely a skeptic until the resurrection), over 500 people at once, and the Apostle himself. This origin of this creed can be traced back to within a decade of the crucifixion, and most of the witnesses were still alive when Paul was writing; the readers could have traveled to Judea to talk to them. This list of witnesses, which includes at least two die-hard skeptics, is overwhelming evidence for the resurrection of Christ.

There is far more evidence in support of the resurrection but even this should convince us that Christ is in fact risen from the dead. That event proves that He was the Son of God. And Christ's nature as the Son of God makes Him an authority in everything he talked about, including the reliability of Scripture as a whole (Matthew 5:18 etc.), the authenticity of the Creation narrative (Matthew 19:4–5; etc.), the coming judgment of the earth (Luke 13:27–30; etc.), and the way of salvation which is available only through Him (John 3:15–16; 14:6).

How does the Bible line up with science?

The tension between current church doctrines, modern scientific perspectives, and the timeless truths of Scripture is an ongoing challenge for anyone searching for Truth in this world. Adding to the difficulty is the fact that the perspectives of scientists are drawn from interpretations of the natural world, while students of Scripture begin with Truths drawn from God's Word. Both approaches are legitimate.

When conflicts occur, great care and patience must be exercised to determine whether scientists or Bible students (if not both together!) have the wrong view of reality. There have been times in history when leaders in the church have had to yield to scientists in their understanding of how poetic or unclear Scriptures relate to the natural world (In the 1600's Galileo clashed with the church regarding a sun-centric solar system. When faced with the scientific evidence the church eventually adjusted its view). There have also been many occasions where scientists have been forced by natural evidence to return to perspectives consistently taught by the Bible (such as human ancestry tracing back to one original couple (Acts 17:26); now proven by genetics).

In short, each conflict between modern scientific opinion and modern theological perspective must be taken case by case. As one who is persuaded of the divine nature and origin of Scripture, I am comfortable with committing to clear teachings in the Bible that go against current scientific opinion. However, I am also comfortable with allowing scientists to challenge long-held perspectives and opinions within the church. If we claim to be followers of the Truth, we must be willing to follow Him wherever He leads!

If the Bible is true then how come there are so many different perspectives on what it really teaches? How can I tell who's right?

Let's begin by stating that there is only one completely right interpretation of Scripture, and it is the one intended by God when He inspired it. While every passage of the Bible is rich and different teachers can emphasize different points, opinions of a particular passage which contradict each other cannot both be right.

It is also helpful to know a couple of facts about the Bible. First is that the Bible was intended to communicate (Hebrews 1:1). Second; the Bible is intended for everyone to read, not just an initiated few, or well-educated experts (Deuteronomy 6:6–9; Psalm 1:1–2; 2 Timothy 3:16–17). Finally, the Bible was written to provide mankind with a standard for right and wrong behavior (Psalm 119:11, 105). These truths require us to start with the most basic or obvious meaning possible in a particular text, and to begin reading the Bible with the same basic rules of literature that we use to read other books (genera, author's intended meaning, etc.).

Now, that doesn't mean that there are not some passages of Scripture that are difficult to interpret, nor does it mean that there aren't deep and profound truths in a passage that we might over-look by ourselves. The more a person knows about the Bible, the more that they are able to learn and share. This is why we all can benefit from those with a deeper understanding of the Bible than we ourselves possess. A good Bible teacher will lay hold of truths that are beyond our reach and bring them down to our level. How-ever, each of us is responsible for understanding God's message as best as we can so that we can respond appropriately in our lives (Matthew 7:24; James 1:22–25; 2 Peter 3:18; 1 John 2:20, 27).

If a teacher presents an interpretation of Scripture that does not seem accurate or contradicts what you've been told in the past, ask them about it (1 Thessalonians 5:21). A good teacher will al-ways be willing to explain their perspective.

Even if we assume that one particular religion is true, doesn't the existence of many religions at least prove that mankind likes to make up religious stories, and that people have a tendency to believe them? How do you know yours isn't one of those?

This question was asked by an antagonistic atheist during a col-lege presentation and forwarded to us by believers. The first thing I would like to point out is that every belief system in the world (including atheism) claims to be exclusively true. The atheist who asked this question believes that his own truth claims are uniquely true and exclusively able to explain reality. The stories that he believes and presents concerning reality (the belief that nothing suddenly exploded into everything, the idea that complex organic systems could blindly and randomly assemble themselves, etc.) are just as prone to the questions he has leveled at Christianity. How do we know that a gullible human race hasn't been fed a pack of lies concerning the big bang and spontaneous generation? How does this man know that what he believes isn't just another blind attempt on the part of the human race to explain the unexplain-able? He believes that his stories are distinct from all other truth claims of the world, and so do we. The question is: whose belief system holds up best under scrutiny?

Let's explore the answer to this question this by examining various creation/origin accounts. Ancient mythologies present highly poetic, irrational, and confusing explanations for the origin of the universe. The ancient Greeks thought the world arose through a conflict between gods and titans; they said the gods came from the titans but had no explanation for where the titans came from! Some Native American legends claim that the earth came into being on the back of a gigantic turtle swimming in a cosmic sea!

Atheists also have various stories that try to explain why there is something rather than nothing. But they all dance around the fundamental fact that everything that begins must have been caused. Space and time have a beginning, so they must have been caused by something/someone who exists outside of space and time, is personal, willful, and extremely powerful. Atheists resist this logical conclusion because it obviously points them in a direction they don't want to go!

In contrast to these stories, Genesis 1 presents a clear and sensible narrative. The complexity of life and the universe is explained by its direct creation at the hands of an omniscient creator, the process laid out in Genesis (planning, execution, evaluation) is remarkably similar to the one used by modern engineers to develop complex systems. After examining the evidence for both sides, I personally became convinced that the perspective taught in Scripture is the most rational perspective of reality available.

Why would a good God allow demons to exist?

Let me begin with some background. For those who don't know, the Bible tells us that there are a multitude of spiritual beings called angels who dwell with God in heaven (Psalm 103:20; Daniel 7:9–10). The Bible also indicates that a powerful angel rebelled against God in the distant past and deceived a third of the angels into joining him (Revelation 12:3–9). These rebels would come to be known as Satan and his demons; the spiritual enemies of God and His people.

Now to the question: why doesn't God just wipe these demons out? If God had crushed the rebellion in its infancy, it might've given the impression that Satan and the demons were a threat to him. It would also have indicated that God rules by brute force rather than divine wisdom and sovereignty. The truth of God's superiority is far more profound. Any created being who tries to stand against God will find themselves pathetically outmatched (2 Samuel 22:27; Job 5:13).

The gospel is the perfect example of this. In the Old Testament God promised to send a Messiah who would crush Satan and end his schemes once and for all (Genesis 3:15). Because of this, Satan was determined to prevent God's plan from reaching fulfillment by any means necessary. When Jesus appeared, Satan threw everything at him that he could muster; temptations (Matthew 4), assassination attempts (Matthew 2:16–18; Luke 4:28–30), and political plots (John 6:15). Finally, Satan corrupted one of Jesus' twelve disciples and arranged for a betrayal, fake trial, and crucifixion (John 13:26–27 & following). However, Satan failed to realize that he was accomplishing God's purpose by slaying God's sinless son as a sacrifice for the sins of the world, thus freeing us from Satan's control (Luke 4:16–21). God tricked Satan into releasing his captives! The gospel was God's ultimate demonstration of superiority over Satan and the demons (Col 2:13–15). Now God only waits for the good news of the gospel to reach throughout the earth before condemning Satan to his fiery punishment (Revelation 20:10).

Why would God allow an immoral couple like Judah and Tamar to be in the genealogy of Christ?

It is a common misconception to think that God only allows perfect, "holy" people to participate in his will. This is backwards; God does not pick holy people to use in His plans; the people he picks are holy because He picked them! Romans 3:10 tells us that no one is righteous, or good enough to meet God's holy standards. If God held tryouts for those seeking to be used by him, or limited his work to 'the right kind of person' He'd be doing all the work Himself because He is the only one qualified.

God's special work in a person's life is not a reward for good behavior, nor is it an indication of any special quality on the part of the chosen (Romans 9:15–16; 1 Corinthians 1:26–29). God chooses to demonstrate His grace and power by blessing, changing, and transforming the most unlikely of people! Judah was a hard man; a murderer who lived only for himself. Yet God shaped this man into a self-sacrificing leader who was even willing to surrender his own freedom for the sake of his young brother Benjamin (Genesis 44:33–34)! It was the leadership that God built into Judah that prepared the way for his descendant: Jesus Christ, who would be the ultimate self-sacrificing leader.

Judah made a chain of very wrong choices in regards to Tamar and the rest of his family, and those choices had consequences. While God neither caused nor condoned Judah's sin, He did a gracious work in his family, redeeming them and preparing them for the work He wanted to do in them and through them. God is willing to take anyone as far in the right direction as they are willing to go and no one has ever messed up so much that God's grace cannot make them better!

How could a loving God command genocide? God told Israel to kill all of the Canaanites; men women and children!

The first question I would have to ask this person is whether they are accusing God of injustice or inconsistency? In order to accuse God of injustice we would have to know more about justice than God does and be powerful enough to hold Him to our point of view. I don't see that happening any time soon.

If our wish is to reconcile God's love and goodness with his sterner commands in the Bible, then we must begin by remembering that the biblical concepts of justice, love, and virtue are all drawn fundamentally from the nature of God. God is love (1 John

4:8), and His character and actions establish the benchmark for justice and virtue (Psalm 33:4–5). Therefore, every act of God is both loving and just by definition, and we must adjust our perspective of these qualities to match God's actions, instead of judging God's actions by our imperfect understanding.

God's Word informs us that we have ruined both God's creation and our own nature (Romans 8:21–22). Even before we are born, we are tainted by sin and deserving of judgment (Psalm 51:5). So then, God has never condemned an innocent to destruction because no one is innocent (Romans 3:10–12)!

I occasionally dabble in (very unskilled) wire art. Let's say I was working on a piece of wire art when it became crushed and ruined. I decide not to throw the piece away and instead try to repair it. While doing so I decide that one part of the project is too far gone, remove it, and start designing a piece to replace it. Do I not have every right to do so as the creator of the project? In the same way, God had determined that the Canaanites had been wholly corrupted by sin and needed to be removed from the earth (Deuteronomy 9:4); He had every right to make that decision. I believe that as we learn true justice and love from God, we come to better understand and appreciate His willingness to make hard choices in order to save those who are still able to be saved.

There are a couple more points that pertain to this discussion: these are the differences between man and God, as well as the nature of the value of human life.

Actions such as genocide are forbidden to human beings because our wisdom, perspective, and character are not sufficient to decide who lives and dies with perfect justice and wisdom. We should not 'play God' because we are not God! However, our Sovereign Creator is fully entitled to remove any gift He has given to us at His own discretion (Job 1:21), and He does so with perfect love, justice, and skill. God does not 'play God;' He *is* God!

How do we reconcile events like the Canaanite judgment with the value the Bible places on human life? Simply by understanding why human life is valuable and who has the right to determine its length. While the Bible does teach that all human life possesses value imputed by our Creator (Genesis 1:27), it also teaches that the length of that life is determined by God; He decides the length of our days and reserves the right to cut our lives short if we give ourselves to corruption, immorality, and sin. In commanding the Israelites to destroy the Canaanites God was simply exercising that authority.

In short, the power of life and death remains in the hands of the only possessor of perfect wisdom and justice, the Lord Himself. And that is precisely where it belongs.

If God created everything, doesn't that mean he created evil?

That would be a logical thought, wouldn't it? Unfortunately, logical conclusions can still be wrong if they are based on faulty or limited information. Let's break your reasoning down into a logical framework of premises and conclusions: God created everything; evil is a thing; therefore, God created evil. The logic is sound but when we check our conclusions against God's perfect Word, we see that one premise is wrong. It is correct to say that God created everything (Revelation 4:11). However, the Bible tells us clearly that God did not create evil, and that he is too holy to even look upon it (Psalm 5:4–6). Which then leads to a different but equally logical conclusion: evil must not be a thing.

This is borne out by Scripture. Just like darkness has no physical form (there are light particles but no dark particles; darkness is just the absence of light), so also evil is any departure or deviation from God's perfect goodness). Evil is called ungodliness or the absence of God (Romans 3:10). Evil is also compared to brokenness (the absence of function or wholeness), sickness (the absence of well-being or health), and unrighteousness (the lack of perfect character).

This question illustrates the importance of using all the tools available to us when seeking to understand our world. Both God and Scripture encourage us to use the logic and reason we've been given to try and understand what is true, real, and good (Isaiah 1:18). However, we've also been given the authoritative word of

God to guide us in our thinking and reasoning (John 17:17). This provides an important check to our thinking, ensuring that we don't get too far off track when seeking the right understanding. Pastors and teachers can also help us to check our conclusions.

Why would God let the Coronavirus pandemic kill so many people?

This is an important question and one that I want to handle with particular care and sensitivity. Probably the best way to do so is to encourage those seeking the answer to this question to read the story of the sickness and death of Lazarus in the Gospel of John, chapter 11. Since Jesus Christ was God Himself, living on the earth as a human being, the way he responded to the death of his good friend Lazarus shows us several important things about God's character. I will present the main points here but I encourage you to read the story to get the full sense of it.

First, we see that Jesus wept when faced with the sorrow of others (John 11:35). From this we can see that God is not distant in our grief and questions; when life causes us pain, He steps off his throne and joins us in our grief (Psalm 147:3). Secondly, God has an eternal plan that transcends our limited perspective (John 11:4, 11, 23–26). Just as children can misunderstand their parent's good intentions on the way to the dentist's office, so we can struggle to understand the goodness of an eternal God. Even death is a small thing in light of eternity! Third, God allows death because he has overcome it through the gospel of Jesus Christ. Jesus told His weeping friends in John 11:25–26, "I am the resurrection and the life, the one who believes in Me, though he may die, he shall live, and he who lives and believes in me shall never die." Death can seem like a very frightening thing, but God wants to help us conquer death through Jesus Christ; Death holds no fear for those who trust in Jesus (1 Cor. 15:55–57).

I heard that the virgin birth was invented by the Church 300 years after Christ lived. Is that true?

The virgin birth of Jesus Christ is a cardinal doctrine of the Church and has been from its beginning. It is clearly taught in Scripture (Matthew 1:18–25; Luke 1:26–37), which was written in the 1st century A.D. within a few decades of Christ's ascension. There is a great deal of extra-biblical evidence to support this, which has persuaded many skeptics down through the years to embrace Christ as Lord and Savior. Yet we still hear of many who claim that Christianity has been proven to be a fraud. Let me take some space here to explain why this is.

There is a large and active body of intellectuals who embrace a mindset that is known as Naturalism. Basically, this group has decided that the world came about through entirely natural means and that all references to historical supernatural events are a result of lying or mythology. Once they become convinced of these ideas, they bring them as assumptions to everything they consider, and these assumptions affect their responses to any given situation.

So then, when naturalists examine a miraculous event like the virgin birth, their preconceived notions about miracles lead them to minimize, explain away, or ignore any evidence that might support the virgin birth, and maximize anything that might discredit it.

We should know, however, that preconceived notions are universal. Christians also have preconceptions that affect our thinking on various subjects. Preconceptions are only bad when they're wrong. If they are wrong then they will warp our thinking until we reexamine our point of view and identify the error.

This is why we hear such different views from educated people on the subject of religion and Christianity. It is a war of ideas and the stakes are high. Each person individually must examine the evidence and decide what the truth is, our eternity rests on how well we make that choice. But God is available to help guide seekers towards a knowledge of the truth (Jeremiah 29:13).

You mentioned "extrabiblical evidence for the virgin birth." Exactly what evidence were you talking about?

What I meant by extrabiblical evidence is that a Christian's faith can be sustained by far more than "The Bible tells me so" in regards to various events and truths proclaimed by Scripture. The Virgin Birth is one of many historical events in Scripture which can rationally be taken at face value.

The evidence for the virgin birth rests fundamentally with two contemporary historical accounts: the gospels of Matthew and Luke. By poring over 5,600 manuscripts of the New Testament (over twice as many as any other ancient work), Bible scholars have ensured that Christians can have complete confidence in the accuracy of our Bible; including the gospels. What we read is what the original authors wrote.

We can have just as much confidence that the gospel authors were honest about what they recorded, as J. Warner Wallace can attest. J. Warner Wallace is a retired, award-winning cold case detective and former atheist. He has closed dozens of cold cases, relying solely on written documents, often cracking a case by identifying false witnesses or missed details in written testimony. This skeptic was sure he could do the same with the gospels, but the more he examined them the more convinced he became that these men were presenting a straightforward account. Their lack of copying from each other, their willingness to present potentially harmful truths, and their commitment to the truth in the face of hardship and death threats all showed him that their accounts could be trusted. He became a Christian as a result of that journey (which you can read about in his book *Cold Case Christianity*). This is only one example of skeptics who were forced to change their views on Christianity by the integrity of the gospel accounts.

A scholar of ancient literature once said this about the accuracy of the New Testament: "To be skeptical of the. . .text of the New Testament is to allow all of classical antiquity to slip into obscurity, for no documents of the ancient period are as well attested bibliographically as the New Testament." (John W. Montgomery,

History and Christianity; Downers Grove, IL, Intervarsity Press 1964, pg. 29). God took care to ensure that Christ's identity and work were validated by miracles like the virgin birth, He saw to it that the events were recorded by eyewitnesses. And He ensured that those eyewitness statements were preserved and distributed so that all could *know* that Jesus really is our Savior (see John 20:30–31).

If the Bible is supposed to be 100 percent true, why do the four gospels give such different accounts of the resurrection? They can't all be right!

Actually, they can! It is extremely common for witnesses of an event to present confusing and (seemingly) contradictory accounts. Police investigators are reassured by this! If they get a bunch of word-perfect, identical accounts, all it proves is that the witnesses agreed on their story before-hand! So then, let's examine some details from these accounts and see if we can't bring them together.

Matthew testifies that Mary Magdalene and "the other Mary" came to the tomb at dawn and found it empty (Matthew 28:1). They saw an angel who had rolled back the stone (Matthew 28:2–4), they then ran to tell the disciples (Matthew 28:8). Mark states that Mary Magdalene, Mary the mother of James, and Salome brought burial spices to the tomb early in the morning, and 'a young man in a white robe' told them Jesus had risen (Mark 16:1–6). Luke records the two Marys and Joanna, among others, coming to the tomb and meeting two men in shining garments (Luke 24:1–4), then they told Peter, who also came to the tomb to look (Luke 24:12). John says that Mary Magdalene alone came to the tomb *while it was still dark*, saw the stone rolled away and ran to tell Peter and John, who both came to see the tomb (John 20:1–8). These witnesses certainly didn't get their story together ahead of time!

However, with a little legwork these accounts harmonize quite nicely. Mary Magdalene comes to the tomb before sunrise and discovers the empty tomb (John 20:1). While running to tell the disciples she meets the other women who were bringing spices to anoint Jesus. All of the women then return to the tomb and see again that it is empty (Notice that John records Mary telling the disciples in John 20:2, "*We* do not know where they laid Him."). They then meet the angel. Matthew and Luke's disagreement regarding how many angels were there can be explained either as describing two events or by Matthew focusing on the angel who spoke (his account seems more concise in general than Luke, so the second option may be preferable). Either way the women return to the disciples, at which point Peter and John come out to the tomb. Luke is only concerned with Peter coming and viewing the cloths (Luke 24:12), but John elaborates and clarifies exactly what happened (John 20:3–8). At no point do the accounts directly contradict each other. Each author relates pertinent details, and the details they share do indeed harmonize with one another to form a consistent and reliable whole.

If God is supposed to be fair and just, why does it seem like he has different standards for different people?

Two words, friend: extenuating circumstances. Just like judges today adjust their verdict to allow for the circumstances of the crime so also God takes all circumstances into account when responding to the sins of the world. Let me list some of the biblical principles which influence God's verdicts.

Romans 5:23 reveals the fundamental law of punishment for sin; that is death. It is what everyone deserves and earns by our disobedience towards God. This reveals to us that God is never too harsh on sin. On the contrary, almost every situation demonstrates God's mercy in withholding full punishment and giving the guilty person grace and a second chance.

Another important thing to understand about God is that he holds all power and authority. In America we are used to separation of powers. It is wrong for an American judge to set aside the law because he has not been given the authority to do so. But God exercises penultimate judicial, executive, and legislative authority at all times and He maintains absolute freedom to manage each situation by His perfect character and justice, unfettered by any restraint (Isaiah 33:22; Romans 9:14–15).

There are many more principles that we could discuss but for sake of space I will include just one more. The fundamental complaint behind this question is that God seems to lay justice aside in certain circumstances and allow the guilty to go free. How can He do that and still be perfectly just and fair? Romans 3:23–26 has the answer. Even though every human being is guilty and deserving of death, God has chosen to provide a way of escape by taking the just punishment for our sins and placing it upon Christ. Those who trust in God's mercy through Christ receive perfect forgiveness of sins, and God remains "both just and justifier of the one who has faith in Christ Jesus," This makes grace through Christ the most important extenuating circumstance of all!

How does God's judgment balance with His love?

It can be difficult to understand how God can exercise perfect love while also carrying out seemingly harsh judgments. But we can reconcile love and judgment simply by recognizing the overlap between them. In other words, the Bible lays out several different ways in which God's love is exercised in judgment, and also to see that His judgment is itself an expression of His love. Let's take a look a couple of examples:

First, Scripture teaches us that the love of God causes Him to limit the extent of his judgment. When we read the passages that set out God's judgment it is easy to forget that our sins merited far greater punishment than God has chosen to mete out (Ezra 9:13; Isaiah 1:9; Lamentations 3:22; Amos 7:1–6). I do not think that we ever have or ever will experience the full extent of God's wrath or judgment. Even in God's final and ultimate judgment His mercy will still shine through (Matthew 24:22).

We can also see God's love in His offer of universal pardon to the world (John 3:16; 1 Timothy 2:3–4). Although He had every excuse to rain down His fury and judgment, God freely chose to provide salvation. The only ones who will feel any part of His wrath are those who spurn His offer of pardon. Truly God does not delight in punishing the wicked (Matthew 9:11–13), but delights in mercy (Micah 7:18).

Often, when God's judgment feels unloving to us it is because we do not understand the danger we are in. Just like a person crossing the street unaware of a speeding car may initially feel anger when they are knocked back onto the sidewalk, so we also can feel anger at God when his wake-up calls finally get our attention. We must come to understand that all of God's motives in judgment are fundamentally loving. They include: attempting to get our attention so that we avoid a more dangerous fate (John 5:14), teaching us to pursue good and healthy things and avoid things that are harmful (Deuteronomy 30:19–20), and a desire to help us understand his mercy (Romans 9:22–23).

I sometimes hear of well-known Christians renouncing their faith. How can this happen? Are they still saved

When a professing believer renounces the faith and walks away from God there are several possible reasons for it. It may be that this person never actually trusted in Christ but lived among Christians as a pretender (1 John 2:19). While practicing good works and trying to blend in, they never experienced genuine regeneration and fell away once they could no longer keep up the charade (Matthew 13:24–30). I also believe that there are cases where a believer's struggles with doubts and questions can cause them to step away from church or the outward exercise of their faith for a time. Their faith in Christ undergoes a severe trial, even to the point that it appears to others that they no longer believe (2 Corinthians 1:8). However, if they are truly saved I believe such people will eventually conquer their doubts and return to fellowship with God and the Church (John 6:39–40; 10:28–30).

The Apostle Paul also had to deal with professing believers departing from the faith. In 2 Timothy he relates to Timothy the news that two of their partners in the ministry had walked away, drawing many after them. Despite this, Paul is able to maintain faith in God and shares the means for doing so with Timothy; it was his confidence that God knows those who truly belong to him and the encouragement for all professing believers to depart from sin (2 Timothy 2:17–19).

While it is difficult to know for sure whether an individual who has apparently departed from the faith is a struggling believer or was never saved (and we really shouldn't try to judge that anyway), there are several promises of Scripture that we can remain confident in regarding the truth of the gospel and our own salvation (John 6:37; 10:28; Romans 8:16; etc.). We can also show compassion and sympathy to those struggling with doubt and questions by remembering the many godly individuals in Scripture who had similar experiences, including Abraham (Gen. 15:7–8), Asaph (Psalm 73:13–17), and the Prophet Habakkuk (Hab. 1:2–4).

If God is sovereign, he could have chosen to let history play out in any way He wanted; why did he allow the human race to get into such a mess and then die to save it? What was the point?

Christian thinkers have fairly consistently held the perspective that God's fundamental purpose in creating the universe was self-expression. Like many human artists God wants to express Himself and reveal His character and nature through His works. God's work in Creation reveals His power and authority (Romans 1:20), His skill and wisdom (Psalm 19:1–2), and His amazing artistry (Psalm 139:14).

The twist came when God allowed His work to become corrupted, ruined, and stolen from Him through sin (Romans 8:20–22). He could have stopped it, but He didn't; why? Again, we have no direct answer but we can make a confident guess based on God's original purpose. By examining how history has played out we can see that certain characteristics of God (namely, his unconditional love, mercy, and grace) have become evident, which otherwise could never have been known. If no one had sinned God could never have shown forgiveness. If we did not disqualify ourselves from deserving love, we would never have realized that God's love is unconditional. If there were no injustice in the world God could not demonstrate His greatness as avenger of the weak and giver of grace to the humble. It is amazing to think that all of the sin, rebellion, and injustice in the world cannot thwart God's intentions for His creation. On the contrary; they help to fulfill it!

That being said, we must be careful not think of ourselves as pawns on God's gameboard. We are much more than that to Him. We are the objects of God's divine love and favor, and we have the privilege of being created to know God and understand His character, grace and goodness by experiencing life with Him (Romans 9:22–24; Philippians 3:8). We have been blessed with the opportunity to both witness and participate in God's greatest work, and are meant to enjoy the show for all eternity as God teaches and demonstrates His greatness to us (John 17:3)!

How can we know for sure that Christ was raised from the dead?

By reading about it in the reliable, historical accounts provided to us in Scripture! Even if you do not yet believe that the Bible is the Word of God you still ought to be persuaded by a fair consideration of the four Gospels: Matthew, Mark, Luke, and John. These historical documents have been analyzed by capable historians and experts for generations. Most of them have come to the following conclusions:

First, the Gospels were written shortly after the events they describe. Archaeologists have discovered thousands of copies of the gospel accounts. The dating and distribution of these copies lead us to an early date for the writing of the books: all four gospels must have been written before the close of the first century. This is not a long enough period for true events to have gradually been lost to myth and legend.

Secondly, the Gospels have all the hallmarks of truthful accounts. Some of these indicators are the inclusion of specific details, accounts that agree in the main facts but differ slightly in the details, and authors who portray themselves in a negative light.

Third, the gospels match well with other historical evidence. We have brief accounts of Jesus from several second-hand, non-Christian sources. All of them mention a miracle worker from Galilee who was crucified and proclaimed risen from the dead. We also know that the apostles boldly proclaimed the risen savior, even in the face of death.

Taken together this evidence is not only compelling; it is overwhelming. No other event in history is as well-attested as the resurrection of Jesus Christ. He is risen! And because He is risen the Bible is true and salvation is available to all who believe!

EPILOGUE
Find What You're Looking for in Church

I WOULD IMAGINE THAT many people who read the title of this conclusion feel some reservations and skepticism about its accuracy. For many, church has not been a fulfilling or rewarding experience. Maybe you've tried church once or twice but never figured out what all the fuss was about. Maybe you've been hurt by Christians or a particular church and swore to never go back. Maybe you attend church every Sunday, but never get anything more out of it than a sore backside from those hard pews! I know very well that all these things can happen. In fact, I've experienced most of them myself. Despite this, it is my earnest desire that you would either begin or continue to pursue a healthy relationship with a good church and godly pastor.

A good church will offer a Christian a sense of belonging, a family to plug into; a place to serve and be served (Acts 20:35). Like all relationships, your relationship with this church will require time and investment on your part. But when we take time to serve and invest in the lives of others, we often find that others are there for us when it's our turn to struggle (Proverbs 11:25). A good church will welcome you, encourage you, challenge you, and walk alongside you in your Christian journey. If you are not a Christian, a good church is an opportunity to see Christians in our element. It is a place to find real people, who are seeking God imperfectly, and relying upon His grace to see us through this crazy life. It's a place to bring your questions, doubts, and struggles. It's where we can go to be shown a picture of God's love and the grace that is available to us in Jesus Christ.

Most churches you visit will be served by a pastor. A good pastor is simply a mature Christian who has been called to care for Jesus' church while He is away (1 Peter 5:2–3). Pastors come in many varieties, and we each go about our ministry in a variety of ways (1 Cor. 3:5–8). You will never find a perfect pastor, and you will never find one without needs and quirks of their own. But if you look hard enough, you will find one who will care for you with the care and compassion of Christ.

Odds are that if you find a church and a pastor like this, then they will be in the best position to help you understand who God is and the relationship He desires to have with you. May God bless and keep you as He guides you back into right relationship with Himself through Jesus Christ and the Body of Christ; which is His Church. Amen.

INDEX

Pastors:

Should I share my problems with my pastor or keep them to myself? Pgs. 10–11

Patience:

Where in the Bible does it talk about how to be more patient? Pgs. 22–23

Prayer:

Can I pray even though I haven't gone to church for a long time? Pgs. 49–50

Can I pray without talking or does it have to be out loud? Pgs. 47–48

How should I pray about something like cancer as a Christian? Pgs. 50–51

I'm not a Christian, can I still pray? Pgs. 48–49

How often should we ask God for what we want? Pgs. 55–56

Proofs for Christianity:

How can we know for sure that Christ was raised from the dead? Pgs. 100–101

How do we know that the Bible isn't just a bunch of religious stories? Pgs. 86–87

How does the Bible line up with science? Pgs. 84–85

If the Bible is true, then why are there so many perspectives on it? Pgs. 85–86

Is there any rational evidence for Christianity? Pgs. 83–84

Is it true that the Church invented the virgin birth of Jesus? Pgs. 93–95

Why do the gospels give different accounts of the resurrection? Pgs. 95–96

See also Science *and* God's Nature

Prophets:

Are there prophets in the world today? Pgs. 79–80

Psalms:

Do the Psalms rhyme in another language? Pgs. 70–71

What does the word *Selah* mean? Pgs. 69–70

Revenge:

What does the phrase, "'Vengeance is mine,' says the Lord" really mean? Pgs. 57–58

Sabbath:

Why was the day of meeting changed to Sunday instead of Saturday? Pgs. 13–14

Salvation:

Before Jesus Christ was born, how were people saved? Pg. 62

If all I have to do to be saved is believe, what incentive is there for me to do good works?

If someone dies without knowing how to be saved, will they still go to heaven?

If you tithe are you more apt to go to heaven? Pg. 19

Does a person have to go to church to be saved?

Someone told me we can't know that we're saved because of Ecclesiastes 3:21. Is that true? Pages 60–61

See also Heaven, Hell, *and* Life after Death

Science:

How does the Bible line up with science? Pgs. 84–85

How do dinosaurs fit into the Bible? Were they on the Ark? Pgs. 75–76

Selah

What does the word "Selah" mean? Pgs. 69–70

Serpent:

Did snakes have legs before Genesis 3:14? Pgs. 68–69

Sin:

If sin is Adam's fault, why are we still punished for it? Pgs. 56–57

Is it sinful to have doubts about God? Pgs. 28–29

Is there an unforgivable sin? Pgs. 16–18

How can I know if I'm sinning? Is there a list somewhere? Pgs. 27–28

Spirit:

What is a spirit? Is it different from your soul? Pg. 76–77

Tithing

If you tithe are you more apt to go to heaven? Pg. 19

Transgenderism:

Does the Bible say anything about transgender people? Pg. 10

Warfare:

Should Christians be soldiers or police officers? Is it always wrong to fight? Pg. 6